W9-AYW-734

Gothenburg

Places:

Groups
Participating in the
Jewish Evacuation:

Gilleleje
Elsinore
Snekkersten
Espergærde
Humlebæk

} — Elsinore Sewing Club

Copenhagen —

{ Mogen's Staffeldt's
Bookshop

Bispebjerg Hospital

The Rockefeller
Institute

Lyngby via Copenhagen — The Lyngby Group

...ager and Amager — "Two Women"

...on and Mons Klint — { The Danish-Swedish
Refugee Service

First Printing

*The author and the publisher are grateful to G. P.
Putnam's Sons for permission to quote passages from
October '43, by Aage Bertelsen. (Copyright 1954, by
Aage Bertelsen.)*

Library of Congress Catalog Card Number: 63-9272
Manufactured in the United States of America
Printed by The Murray Printing Co., Forge Village, Mass.
Bound by American Book Stratford Press, New York.

RESCUE
IN DENMARK

by Harold Flender

Simon and Schuster • New York • 1963

To all of the Danish people—those whose names appear in this book and those whose names do not.

Contents

7

Part Four THE AFTERMATH

Preface

As THE Eichmann trial unfolded, I found that the story of the Nazi horror, despite its familiarity, had not lost its power to shock. What particularly depressed me was the reminder of the apathy and toleration—and sometimes approval—of the Nazi bestiality by many of the people of the occupied countries, including Austria, Poland, Czechoslovakia and the Ukraine. The roll call of shame was long and embraced much of Europe.

And then one day, during the trial, mention was made of Denmark and how this small country had saved virtually its entire Jewish population during World War II. The mention was short, the facts brief. In October 1943, the Nazis decided to round up Denmark's eight thousand Jews for shipment to the death camps. The entire country acted as an underground movement to ferry the eight thousand to Sweden. It was one of the few times that Eichmann had been frustrated. He visited Copenhagen in a rage—but to no avail. The Jews were saved.

Most of the story told at the trial came from a Danish Jew who had himself been smuggled to Sweden and who happened to be in Israel at the time of the trial and so was able to testify. He was David Melchior, son of the Chief Rabbi of Denmark. When he completed his testimony, Judge Moshe

Landau turned to Judge Itzak Raveh and said, "This was indeed an intermezzo."

To me, David Melchior's testimony was more than an intermezzo. It was a single beam of light from an otherwise dark continent.

I told my friend Arnold Forster how moved I was by young Melchior's testimony, and Arnold gave me a book to read—*October '43*, written by Aage Bertelsen, a Danish pastor and schoolteacher. It told how Bertelsen and his wife were involved with an underground student organization that was responsible for getting hundreds of Danish Jews to Sweden. Mr. Bertelsen had a simple answer when asked why he had risked his life to aid the Jews: "These people were in mortal danger and we had no alternative. We had to do what we did."

Reading *October '43* confirmed what I had suspected: the story of the Danish rescue of the Jews was a welcome testament of man's humanity to man. I felt that it offered a note of hope to offset the despair evoked by the Eichmann trial testimony and that it should have as wide an audience as possible. My first thought was to present the story on television as a documentary film.

I took the idea to Richard Siemanowski, the producer of the CBS-TV religious program *Look Up and Live*. He approved. We went to Denmark on August 14, 1961, and started researching the story. At first, it was difficult to get the Danes to cooperate: they were silent heroes. Most of them felt that there was nothing extraordinary or unusual in what they had done. Mogens Fisker, a Dane who had helped many Jews to escape, spoke for this group when he described the rescue as "simply the human thing to do." They could see no point in the story being told widely. A smaller group was aware that the Danes had behaved toward the Jews in a manner very different from that of the other Europeans, but they were afraid that talking about it would cheapen what they had done. They were against any form of publicity, commercialization or exploitation. It took a good deal of arguing and cajoling to convince them to cooperate in putting before a television audience at least one example of human behavior during the years of inhumanity.

We finally made our film, using persons and places that had actually been involved in the rescue. "An Act of Faith" was shown in two parts on November 19 and 26, 1961. It received such an unusually warm response from critics and viewers that both parts were repeated together on December 31. In addition, the Anti-Defamation League of B'nai B'rith edited a half-hour version which was made available to religious, civic and educational institutions.

The response to the film was most gratifying. I knew, however, that it had merely scratched the surface of the story. It deserved a fuller, more definitive treatment, such as could be done only in a book. *October '43* was a good document, but it told the story of the activities of only one rescue group the Lyngby Group. I wanted to tell the story of all of the major groups.

In February 1962, I returned to Denmark and spent several months talking to dozens of the rescuers as well as the rescued. In addition, with the aid of translators, I went through all of the available books, articles and archives on the subject in Danish and German.

This book is the result. I have not been able to include all of the names that should be included. To do so would require a volume of smaller print and larger size than the Manhattan telephone directory, for virtually the entire Danish population participated in the rescue of the Jews.

On the outskirts of Jerusalem stands a large building known as Yad Vashem. It is a monument to the atrocities perpetrated against the Jews during World War II. It is a necessary reminder, as was the Eichmann trial, of the depths of depravity to which mankind is capable of sinking. Perhaps now is the time for another type of monument—one dedicated not to despair but to hope, not to death but to life. This monument would be a reminder of those who risked and often sacrificed their lives that others might have their allotted time on earth. Not all monuments need be of stone or marble. Perhaps the longest-lasting monuments are those in the minds and hearts of men. To that purpose this story of the Danish rescue of the Jews is dedicated.

NEW YORK, 1963   H. F.

From the beginning to the end there is only one hero—the people.

—Jules Michelet

ON THE MORNING of Friday, September 30, 1943, Rabbi Marcus Melchior stood before the Holy Ark of the 110-year-old Copenhagen Synagogue.

It was the day before Rosh Hashana, the Jewish New Year. About 150 members of the congregation were present. They were puzzled by the fact that Rabbi Melchior was not in his rabbinical robes.

"There will be no service this morning," said Rabbi Melchior. "Instead, I have very important news to tell you. Last night I received word that tomorrow the Germans plan to raid Jewish homes throughout Copenhagen to arrest all the Danish Jews for shipment to concentration camps. They know that tomorrow is Rosh Hashana and our families will be home. The situation is very serious. We must take action immediately. You must leave the synagogue now and contact all relatives, friends and neighbors you know are Jewish and tell them what I have told you. You must tell them to pass the word on to everyone they know is Jewish. You must also speak to all your Christian friends and tell them to warn the Jews. You must do this immediately, within the next few minutes, so that two or three hours from now everyone will know what is happening. By nightfall tonight we must all be in hiding."[1]

Part One

THE OCCUPATION

Chapter 1   HITLER'S CANARY

Denmark, your people and your country,
Based upon freedom and happiness,
Built on the sand of promises,
Slipping away piece by piece . . .

—KARL ROOS

AT 3:30 A.M. on April 9, 1940, Danish General Staff Headquarters in Copenhagen received the first of several telephone calls that were to affect radically the history of Denmark for the next five years. This first call was from the frontier and reported that "a heavy noise of engines" could be heard along the passage from Rends to Arentoft. The second telephone call was at 4:30 A.M. German troops were reported to have crossed the frontier at Krusaa. Five minutes later the Naval Command announced that German soldiers had disembarked at Assens, Middelfart and Nyborg. At 4:32 A.M. the General Staff was told that German forces had come ashore at Korsør. During the next hour reports poured in with such rapidity that all telephone lines at Staff Headquarters were jammed. At 4:32 A.M. General Prior, commander in chief of Denmark's armed forces, was awakened at his residence at Kastellet and was told to report

to the War Ministry.[1] There, he learned that German troops
and planes had crossed the Danish frontier, that the German
Ambassador had handed a note to the Danish Foreign Minister to the effect that German forces were taking over the
protection of Denmark in order to prevent a British violation
of Danish territory, and that the King, Vice-Admiral and
ministers were meeting at Amalienborg Castle to discuss the
German demand for capitulation.

Before leaving for Amalienborg Castle, General Prior
called to arms the guard at Amalienborg, and ordered all
units throughout Zealand to resist the Germans. All airfields
were to be mobilized. Airmen were to take off from the
airfield at Værløse and were to engage any enemy aircraft
encountered.

By the time General Prior reached Amalienborg Castle,
soldiers of the Danish Guard were firing upon German
troops in the Palace Square. General Prior, opposing sub-
mission, suggested that the King and government leave for
the nearby military camp at Høvelte to continue the fighting.
The King, Premier Stauning and Foreign Minister Munch
rejected this proposal. At 6 A.M. the German demands were
agreed to and the King ordered a cease-fire at the Palace
Square.

General Prior returned to the War Ministry, where he
reluctantly ordered armed forces throughout the country to
cease all further resistance. In less than two hours Denmark
had capitulated. Her nine hundred years of uninterrupted
freedom and independence were at an end. For the next five
years Denmark was to be occupied by Germany.

It was Winston Churchill who called Denmark "the sadis-
tic murderer's canary."[2] But if, at the beginning, Hitler kept
Denmark a well-fed, pampered and spoiled canary, it was
because Denmark behaved as a loving pet perfectly willing to
be caged.

A comparison of Danish armed forces between 1914–18 and 1939–40 shows how much less concerned Denmark was about Hitler's Germany than about the Germany of the Kaiser. In 1914, Denmark had 55,000 men under arms, a number which in the course of four years was gradually reduced to 28,000, as the danger decreased. At the outbreak of World War II in 1939, Danish troops numbered 36,000. Within the next six months, in spite of the fact that the danger had increased, the number of troops was reduced to 14,000.

It has been argued by some that the Danes had no idea that they would be invaded by Germany and that all they wanted was to maintain the neutrality they had enjoyed during World War I. This is a specious argument: the Danes well knew Germany's intentions toward their country. As early as March 2, 1935, the Gothenburg *Trade and Shipping Gazette* wrote: "The German High Command has long been studying the problem of Germany's food supplies in war. Since the Reich's farming output is insufficient to meet the requirements of both army and civilian population, and in view of the fact that the outcome of the war may ultimately depend on food supplies, General Goering has worked out a plan which aims at the occupation of Denmark and Lithuania by German troops directly war breaks out. Under this scheme, which is based on the experiences of the Great War, both countries, after complete occupation, are to be used as German larders (*Kriegsküchen*). North Schleswig and Memel are to serve as pretexts for the invasion of Denmark and Lithuania respectively. The plan, which was worked out upon the initiative of General Goering down to the last detail, has been approved by Herr Hitler and the General Staff."

On July 23, 1938, to insure the success of the plan he had worked out several years earlier, Goering paid a personal visit to Denmark on his yacht *Carin II*, escorted by two German warships, a torpedo boat and a mine sweeper.[3] At Nyborg

Fjord, Goering's yacht discharged two Mercedes Benz
limousines whose passengers were German intelligence officers. While the yacht sailed between Nyborg and Copenhagen, the two limousines followed it on shore. The German
intelligence officers were thus able to examine both the sea
and land fortifications around the coast of Zealand. During
the next few days of Goering's tour through Denmark, the
Danish people gave him an icy welcome. Accustomed to their
king's traveling with no escort, they jeered at Goering, who
was constantly surrounded by a private bodyguard of five
Gestapo men.

The Danish government's attitude toward Goering did not
reflect the antipathy shown him by the people. The government offered no opposition to Goering's inspection tours. It
did not protest or do anything to discourage his being cheered
on the quays and along the roads by the members of the
German colony in Denmark, which included several thousand Germans who years earlier had been adopted by the
Danes as World War I orphans. The government was timid
about doing or saying anything that might offend Germany.
It was this very same attitude that had caused the Danish
government as early as 1934 to close down a Danish anti-Nazi
satirical magazine.[4]

From the earliest days of the Nazi regime, Denmark had
done virtually nothing to protect itself against German invasion. The only fortifications of any consequence in the
entire country had been built on the country's west coast,
facing England. These served as a warning that Denmark was
ready to protect its neutrality against England, if not against
Germany. Along the German border, no preparations had
been made to mine bridges or to block roads. Despite rumors
of German plans to attack Norway and Denmark during the
days preceding April 9, 1940, and even though the Army
Command demanded it, no mobilization had been called, not
even of the security forces. The Army had also asked for

troop concentration, or at least shallow groupings of units along the frontier, but the War Ministry had refused to grant this. Even the frontier gendarmery did not receive troop support. All along the German border no defense fortifications had been built, not a single spadeful of earth dug.

The Danish Navy was even less prepared for war than the Army. The Army, at least, managed to engage in skirmishes with German troops in Jutland, and the Royal Guard fired upon German soldiers at Amalienborg Castle. Thirteen Danish soldiers were killed, twenty-three wounded. But the Navy suffered not a single casualty, and no Danish naval vessels or shore batteries opened fire on German troopships despite the fact that they entered the Danish harbors within point-blank range of Danish naval guns.[5]

No wonder Colonel R. Mikkelsen of the Danish Army answered Danish poet Kaj Munk's query, "When we spoke without being heard, did we then shout? And when that did not help either, did we then shoot?" with the bitter reply: "No, we neither shouted nor shot, we lulled ourselves into a happy-go-lucky attitude, and we had, in other words, the government we deserved."

Norway was invaded the same day as Denmark—April 9, 1940—and it is interesting to compare the reactions of the two governments.

King Christian X of Denmark conceded to German demands almost immediately. General Kurt Himer, chief of the German task force in Denmark, recorded his meeting with the King: "The seventy-year-old King appeared inwardly shattered, although he preserved outward appearances perfectly and maintained absolute dignity during the audience. His whole body trembled. He declared that he and his government would do everything possible to keep peace and order in the country and to eliminate any friction between the German troops and the country. He wished to spare his country further misfortune and misery."[6]

The King of Norway, on the other hand, responded in quite another manner. Haakon VII, who, incidentally, was the brother of Christian X, told his ministers on April 9, 1940 that "if the government should decide to accept the German demands—and I fully understand the reasons in favor of it, considering the impending danger of war in which so many Norwegians will have to give their lives—if so, abdication will be the only course open to me."[7]

The Norwegian government backed its king by calling upon Norway's three million inhabitants to resist the invaders for as long as possible. And resist they did.[8] At Bergen Harbor, Norwegian naval batteries badly damaged the German cruiser *Koenigsberg*. At Kristiansand, on the south coast, shore batteries twice drove off a German fleet led by the cruiser *Karlsruhe*. The severest naval blow dealt the Germans was at the entrance to Oslo Harbor, where Norwegian naval guns sank the heavy cruiser *Bluecher*, with the loss of 1,600 German lives, and severely damaged the battle cruiser *Leutzow*. In cooperation with Britain's Royal Navy, Norway's naval forces played their part in destroying ten German destroyers, three cruisers, two battle cruisers and one pocket battleship. The Germans employed the bulk of their fleet attacking Norway. Thanks largely to Norwegian resistance, German naval losses were so severe that OKH, the German General Staff Headquarters, found them an insurmountable handicap in planning Operation Sea Wolf, the invasion of England, several months later.[9]

The Norwegian Army, together with British, French and Polish forces, inflicted over five thousand casualties upon the invading German Army.

In considering the difference in reactions between the Danes and Norwegians to the German invasions of their countries, it is important to remember the contrast in the

geography of the two countries. Norway, especially in the
north, is a mountainous and heavily wooded country, afford-
ing many opportunities for hiding and for guerilla warfare.
Denmark, on the other hand, is completely flat and open,
offering none of the natural defense advantages of Norway.
Denmark was an easy prey for Hitler's *Panzer* divisions. Still,
many Danes felt that this was no excuse for the almost total
lack of resistance and immediate capitulation to the Germans
by the Danish government.

On April 10, 1940, Colonel Mikkelsen said to his troops:
"Never had soldiers had to fight under more unequal circumstances. Not even a hole in which to die were you allowed
to dig. But by your behavior you have cried out to the whole
Danish people, nay, to all peoples: It was not the Danish
soldier who was at fault, others were to blame . . ."

Who were the others? The government, and—according to
Colonel Mikkelsen—the people. "There was not—and this
was the lack most gravely felt by the Army—a unanimous
Danish people standing behind it in this fatal hour of the
country," he later wrote.

Even those who in 1943 were to risk their lives in the
rescue of the Jews were in 1940 relatively unconcerned about
the German invasion of their country. Their change in attitude, from naïveté and apathy in April 1940 to a readiness to
risk their very lives to aid the Jews in October 1943, is typical
of the change that took place among large segments of the
Danish population once the Germans decided to destroy
Denmark's Jewry.

The original acceptance of the Germans by the Danes,
and their early willingness to allow the Germans into their
country, inspired Hitler to refer to Denmark as a *Muster-
protektorat*, or model protectorate. Here lies part of the
reason why the Danish Jews were allowed their complete
freedom. The Danes had been friendly to the Germans, and,
in appreciation, the Germans were considerate to the Danes.

Christian X was permitted to remain head of state, the Danish Parliament and courts were allowed to function, the Nuremberg edicts against the Jews were not introduced in Denmark.

It was different in Norway. Because of the Norwegian resistance, the Germans instituted an immediate campaign of terror against the Jews: civil rights were abolished, property was seized, identification cards were stamped with the Star of David, searches and arrests were instituted.[10] Thanks to Norway's long frontier with its Scandinavian neighbor, about 800 of Norway's 1,700 Jews were able to escape to Sweden. Of the remaining 900 Norwegian Jews, only twelve escaped death at the hands of the Germans.[11]

In addition to Denmark's early cooperation with Germany, there is still another reason why Hitler had a soft spot in his heart for Denmark: he considered the Danes pure Nordics, since they were descended from the same stock who had inhabited the Danish islands from before the Stone Age. The Kimbric peninsula, Jutland, was the birthplace of the Teutons and the Gottons, and the Danes were blood brothers to the Germans, according to National Socialist philosophy.

Danish cooperation and Nazi racial theories explain, in part, Germany's indulgent attitude toward Denmark, including the exceptional freedom for Danish Jews. But there is still another factor, considerably more important. Before instituting anti-Jewish measures in the countries they occupied, the Germans tried to ascertain to what extent their actions would be supported by the non-Jewish populations of these countries. In Poland and Slovakia, for example, their research revealed that they could start Jewish persecution at any time with impunity. Not only would the Poles and Slovaks refrain from protest, they would help. The Ukrainians outdid the Nazis in slaughtering the local Jewry. The numerous Polish and Slovak atrocities against the Jews and the Ukrainian massacre of 100,000 Jews at Babi Yar are proof of the accuracy of the German predictions. In most of the countries under their domination, the Germans reached the conclusion that arrest and internment of the Jews would meet with little or no opposition.

Their research revealed only one outstanding exception: Denmark.

Chapter 2 LEGACY

Suddenly each man knew what he owed
To his good Danish name.

—KAJ MUNK

THE FIRST GERMAN PLENIPOTENTIARY in Denmark during the occupation was the former ambassador, Cecil von Renthe-Fink. Repeatedly the Foreign Office officials in Berlin concerned with Jewish matters in Scandinavia prodded Renthe-Fink about the embarrassing fact that eight thousand Jews were living freely in a country occupied by the Nazis. There are a series of memoranda on file from "Jewish experts" Werner von Grundherr and Karl Rademacher to Renthe-Fink on this matter.[1] In reply, he warned Berlin that any tampering with the Danish Jews' civil rights would result in a violent reaction on the part of the Danes that could do much harm to the otherwise peaceful relations between the two countries. The furthest he would go was to recommend that Jewish firms in Denmark be deprived of their allocations of coal and fuel from Germany.[2]

The Germans were aware that Renthe-Fink was a diplomat rather than a *Reichskommissar*, and, as such, possibly prejudiced against Hitler's plan to make Europe *"Judenfrei."* In

28

November 1942, they replaced him with Dr. Werner Best, former administrative chief of the Gestapo.. A Gestapo officer of such high rank was not expected to harbor any sentimental notions about Jews. Nevertheless, Best's reports echoed the warnings of Renthe-Fink. Denmark was supplying Germany with enormous quantities of foodstuffs, even more than had been called for by the heavy quotas, and Danish factories were turning out much-needed marine diesel engines as well as parts for airplanes and armored vehicles. If the steady flow of these vital materials was to be uninterrupted, it would be advisable, warned Best, for the Germans to forget about the Danish Jews for a while.

When Ribbentrop objected, Best suggested that if something *had* to be done, perhaps individual Jews could be arrested for political or criminal activities, or Jews could be removed from Danish political life by having them reported to the Danish government as uncooperative. In addition, German firms could refuse to do business with Danish companies owned fully or partially by Jews. More stringent anti-Jewish measures than thése, advised Best, would result in severe anti-German repercussions.[3]

To make sure that Renthe-Fink and Best had correctly interpreted the Danes' attitude toward anti-Semitism, the Foreign Office in Berlin sent to Denmark from Poland, where he had devised the torture instruments used at Auschwitz, Gestapo Colonel Rudolph Mildner. Here was a proven anti-Semite. In effect, his reports paralleled those of Renthe-Fink and Best. When Gestapo headquarters in Berlin expressed incredulity, Mildner flew to Berlin to convince Ribbentrop that hatred of anti-Semitism was endemic to Denmark, and that the Danes would not tolerate persecution of the Jews. He further pointed out that some German soldiers had even become "infected" by the atmosphere of racial and religious tolerance in Denmark, and might not be willing to cooperate in drastic anti-Semitic measures.[4]

As late as the beginning of 1943, while the Gestapo was demanding the arrest and deportation of the Jews, the Foreign Ministry replied by citing the dangers of such an operation. Eberhard von Thadden, one of Eichmann's aides, testified at Nuremberg: "I know that the Foreign Ministry adopted the attitude that . . . deportation of the Jews was politically unacceptable."[5]

Throughout the early years of the occupation, German representatives in Denmark kept sending back to Berlin a large number of reports indicating that, unlike the populations of the other occupied countries—especially Austria, Poland, Czechoslovakia, Hungary and the Ukraine—the Danish population would not tolerate—indeed, would revolt against—persecution of the Jews. And so, to avoid incurring what they knew would be resistance on the part of the Danish people, the Germans allowed the Danish Jews to have their freedom until the fall of 1943.

One cannot help but wonder what the situation might have been for the Jews of the other occupied countries if the peoples of these countries had been as forthright in their opposition to anti-Semitism as the Danes.

Why did the Danes, in contrast to so many other European peoples, find anti-Semitism so unacceptable? "The laws of conscience, though we ascribe them to nature, actually come from custom," wrote Montaigne. And this is as true of the Danes as it is of us all. The opposition to anti-Semitism was part of a custom, a tradition, going back to 1690, when a Danish police chief was relieved of his duties for daring to suggest that Denmark should follow the example of other European countries and establish a ghetto in Copenhagen. The Danish Parliament had immediately followed the dismissal of the police chief by passing a resolution condemning the very idea of a ghetto as "an inhuman way of life." The Danish custom of human rights was further established in 1814, a year when slavery was still very much alive in the

United States, by the passage of a bill in the Danish Parliament making *all* racial and religious discrimination punishable by law.

But Renthe-Fink, Best and Mildner did not need a course in Danish history to be so certain of the Danes' opposition to anti-Jewish measures. They had numerous signs before their very eyes.

There were the stories circulating about King Christian X. It was said that when Renthe-Fink used the phrase "Jewish question," the King replied, "There is no Jewish question in this country. There is only my people." Another story had it that when German officials reproached King Christian for his "negligence of the Jewish problem," he coldly answered, "Gentlemen, since we have never considered ourselves inferior to the Jews, we have no such problem here." A favorite story was that King Christian had announced, "If the Germans want to introduce the yellow Jewish star in Denmark, I and my whole family will wear it as a sign of the highest distinction."

Many Danes spread stories that the King and members of his family had actually worn the yellow Star of David, and by doing so caused the Germans to rescind the order that all Danish Jews were to wear the armband.

Actually, none of these stories is true.[6] King Christian X never made the statements attributed to him. He never wore the armband, never even said that he would wear it. Having been advised of the Danes' intense antipathy to anti-Semitism, the Germans never attempted or even threatened to introduce the yellow Star of David in Denmark. That historical and popular accounts of the German occupation of Denmark have repeated the erroneous stories of King Christian X and the yellow Star of David is no grave historical error. The stories are apocryphal, but they are an indication of what the Danish people *wanted* to believe about their king. As such, these tales reflect the attitude of the bulk of the Danish people toward the Jews.

Apart from the popular stories about the King, the Germans had other evidence of Danish opposition to anti-Semitism. An anti-Semitic Danish newspaper the Germans started publishing in Copenhagen, modeled after Julius Streicher's *Der Stürmer*, had to shut down for lack of subscribers. Exhibitions of anti-Semitic literature and showings of anti-Semitic films had to be discontinued because they were virtually unattended.

Early in 1942, having read of German atrocities against the Jews of other occupied countries, a number of physicians on the staff of Bispebjerg Hospital circulated a petition among all of the doctors affiliated with the hospital, declaring, among other things, that the physicians who signed it would continue to support the Danish government, provided the Danish government would allow no persecution of Danish Jews. Of the seventy-five physicians who saw the petition, sixty-four signed it.

When Werner Best questioned Prime Minister Erik Scavenius about the possible introduction of anti-Semitic measures in 1942, Scavenius replied that should such measures be introduced, he and his entire cabinet would resign in protest.

Late in 1942 an attempt was made to set fire to the Copenhagen Synagogue. As in an abortive attempt that took place in 1941, it was prevented by the Danish Police. The only damage the Germans had been able to accomplish was the painting of swastikas on the Synagogue walls. To prevent further attempts at the destruction of the Synagogue, the Danish Police formed a special auxiliary police unit, composed of Danish Jews armed with clubs and guns. The sole assignment given to this auxiliary unit was the guarding of the Synagogue. As a further preventive measure, the Danish

Police devised an electric warning syste
nection between the Synagogue and P

In January 1943, at a student festiv
ish students announced that they
audience to participate in the singir
anthems of countries dear to the
Germans present were not at all s
presented was the Danish natio
startled and chagrined when, f
instead of hearing, as they ma
über Alles," the Zionist flag
students sang "Hatikvah," t

The Danish Jews were
their fellow Danes of N
confidence and, later, in
to their friends, their
for aid. Their attitude
so many eastern Eur
at the Eichmann
tempted to escape
turn? We knew
While the Da
was beneficial
same time, a f
be seen ever
Christian w
ment and
continued
as free
had not
the er
lives.

Part Two

THE RAID

Chapter 3 THE GERMANS
CHANGE THEIR MINDS

*If the international Jewish financiers within and with-
out Europe succeed in plunging the nations once more
into a world war, then the result will not be the
Bolshevization of the world and thereby the victory
of Jewry—but the annihilation of the Jewish race in
Europe.*

—ADOLF HITLER, *Speech before the Reichstag,*
January 30, 1939

IN 1943 THE GERMANS changed their minds
about Denmark's Jews. What brought about the change?
First, the obsessive nature of Hitler's racist theories, at the
dark heart of which lay his insistence upon total annihilation
of world Jewry. The "Final Solution" allowed no exceptions.
It was unthinkable to him that Jews should be allowed to
maintain their freedom in Denmark, a country occupied by
German troops.

Secondly, the Danes, to a large extent because of Nazi anti-
Semitism, were becoming disenchanted with the Germans.
Their violent protests brought about German reprisals, and

gave the Nazis an excuse to end the freedom of the Jews in
Denmark.

Mrs. Gethe Kisling, a nurse, was typical of the large number of Danes who, accepting the idea of Danish collaboration
with Germany in 1940, had come to oppose the Germans in
1943 because of their anti-Semitism. "Worst of all was learning what the Germans had done to the Jews in Norway,
Holland and the other countries," explained Mrs. Kisling.
"We wondered whether they would attempt to do anything
like that with our Jews. As time went on we became more
and more annoyed by the situation. A strong feeling of hate
began to build up in most people and a desire to be allowed
to do something to fight the enemy instead of just having to
behave."

Others began opposing the Germans in the summer of
1943 for less idealistic reasons, such as the growing food
shortage and the fact that the Allies had clearly begun to win
the war.

Professor of neurology Mogens Fog, one of the earliest of
the underground resistance fighters, made a secret broadcast
in the summer of 1943 in which he said: "Like a cutting irony
stand today the proud words of Johannes V. Jensen: 'The
Danes could never take being suppressed.' I would say that
as long as there is food enough they could take being suppressed quite well."

Suddenly, there was not food enough. What had started as
a boom in exports for the Danes was now becoming a strain
on the economy. The Germans were draining the country
dry, and the Danes, who rival the French in their love of
lavish dining, were suddenly faced with serious food shortages. More important, the tide of German victories was turning. By the summer of 1943, German forces had suffered
catastrophic defeats at Stalingrad and El Alamein. In July
1943, Sicily was invaded by the Allies and Mussolini was
overthrown.

The sudden upsurge of "incidents" involving Danes and Germans can be seen by a perusal of the newspapers of July 1943. On July 13, six Danes were sentenced to thirty days' imprisonment for molesting and insulting German officers and soldiers. A fifty-year-old man was sentenced to thirty days for insulting a detachment of German soldiers on the march. Another man got thirty days for having written the French word *victoire* on a German signboard. On July 18, a previous offender was sentenced to sixty days' imprisonment for having molested a German soldier accompanied by a Danish woman. On July 19, a youth, aged eighteen, got thirty days in prison for insulting Germans on the march.

On July 20, a man was sent to prison for thirty days for spreading rumors that the Germans had confiscated copper and sent it to Germany; a worker, aged forty, got thirty days' imprisonment for having addressed a German soldier in English; a middle-aged man was sentenced to two years in prison for having "libeled" Hitler and the German people in a letter to the local German commander; a man, aged twenty-two, got twenty days' imprisonment for conspicuously extinguishing a cigarette on a signboard belonging to the German Wehrmacht; and a man, aged thirty-seven, was sentenced to forty days' imprisonment for having, while intoxicated, insulted and molested a German soldier.

In August of 1943, Best was ordered to Berlin to report before the Führer himself. Hitler told him that the idea of Danish Jews walking around free was "loathsome."[1] When Best referred to the possible dire consequences of anti-Jewish actions, Hitler replied that the Danes seemed to be resisting despite the lack of anti-Jewish measures, and, if conditions got worse, a state of military emergency would have to be declared in which the reins of government would be handed over to the military commander, General von Hannecken.

Best returned to Denmark "pale and shaken."[2]

August 1943, was a bad month for him. If he had been left "pale and shaken" by his meeting with Hitler, increased Danish resistance was soon to leave him completely distraught.

Workers' groups began to protest with a series of strikes in the shipyards of Copenhagen and Odense. To handle the strikers, the Germans recalled from the Russian front the "Schalburg Corps," Danish pro-Nazis who had volunteered to fight for Hitler in the east, and instructed them to deal with their fellow Danes. The appearance on the streets of Copenhagen of these Danish traitors—they were mainly criminals freed from prison by the Germans—infuriated the Danes. What had been until then strikes confined to the ship-yards became general strikes throughout the city. At one of these demonstrations, a German officer opened fire on the strikers, and a group of them turned upon him in fury and beat him to death.

Whatever the causes—hatred of the Nazi ideology, anger over food shortages, realization that the Allies would win the war, rage at the Germans' trying to set Dane against Dane—the Danes began actively to oppose Germany in August 1943. To crush the growing resistance, the Germans delivered an ultimatum to the Danish government on August 28, 1943:

The Danish government shall declare, with immediate effect, a state of emergency in the entire country. This state of emergency shall include the following provisions:

1. Prohibition of public gatherings exceeding five persons.
2. Prohibition of strikes and any kind of financial support to strikers.
3. Prohibition of any gatherings whether indoor or outdoor. Curfew to be imposed as from 8:30 P.M. All firearms and explosives not yet seized to be delivered up before the first of September, 1943.
4. Prohibition of any annoyance of Danish citizens owing to

the cooperation by them or their relatives with the German
authorities or their connections with the Germans.
5. Censorship of the press to be imposed in cooperation with the
Germans.
6. Setting up of promptly functioning Danish special tribunals for
dealing with infringement to suffer the severest punishments
compatible with the emergency act according to which the
government is empowered to enforce any measures required
for the maintenance of law and order.

Sabotage and any incitement thereto, attacks on units of the
Wehrmacht or on single members thereof, possession of firearms
or explosives after the first of September, 1943, shall be immediately punishable by death.

The Reich government expects the acceptance of these demands
by the Danish government before 4 P.M. today.

COPENHAGEN, August 28, 1943.[3]

Best waited in vain for acceptance of the German ultimatum. The Danish government, after three years of peaceful
cooperation with the invaders, flatly rejected the German
demands, and King Christian X congratulated his government
on its decision.

What Best least of all wanted—a state of military emergency—was finally declared in Denmark. In addition, Hitler
removed him as plenipotentiary and replaced him with General von Hannecken. On the morning of August 29, 1943,
the citizens of Copenhagen awoke to find German soldiers
posted outside all government buildings, telephone and mail
services temporarily halted and the radio incessantly broad-
casting a proclamation by Hannecken:

The latest events have shown that the Danish government is
no longer capable of maintaining law and order in Denmark.
The disturbances provoked by foreign agents are aimed directly
at the Wehrmacht. Therefore, in accordance with the articles
Nos. 42–56 of the Hague Convention of the laws and customs of

war on land, I declare a military state of emergency in the whole of Denmark.

With immediate effect I decree as follows:

1. Civil servants shall loyally continue in the performance of their duties. They shall comply with the directions given by the appointed competent German authorities.
2. Assemblage of crowds and gatherings of more than five persons in the streets and in public or in private are forbidden.
3. Closing hours shall be at nightfall. As from the same hour a curfew is imposed.
4. The use of the mail, telegraph or telephone is prohibited until further notice.
5. A ban is imposed on all strikes. Inducements to strikes which would cause disadvantages to the Wehrmacht are acts furthering the interests of the enemy and are punishable by death.

Offences against the above decrees will be dealt with by German special tribunals.

Arms will be ruthlessly used against acts of violence, assemblage of crowds, etc.

Any Danish citizen who complies with the international law of war on land will enjoy the protection of his person and property according to the law.

COMMANDER-IN-CHIEF,
REICH FORCES IN DENMARK

To insure the effectiveness of the proclamation, the Germans took as hostages hundreds of prominent Danes, including high-ranking army and navy officers. No longer the plenipotentiary, now only second in command, Best nevertheless felt obliged to make some display of authority. On the afternoon of August 29, 1943, he called a press meeting of Danish newspaper editors, and told them that "in this ridiculous little country, the press has inoculated the people with the idea that Germany is weak . . . The proclamation issued during the night is our answer. From now on, each editor will be responsible with his head for seeing that the people are no longer poisoned."[4]

As a reaction to the new German measures, a number of things occurred. Danish newspapermen formed one of the best underground newspaper organizations in any of the occupied countries. The King declared himself a prisoner of war. The cabinet resigned and Parliament dissolved itself. The Danish armed forces used rifles, grenades and light machine guns to hold off the German attack on the Copenhagen Navy Yard long enough for Rear Admiral Vedel to run up this signal on the main of his flagship, the forty-year-old coast defense vessel *Peder Skram:* "Scuttle or escape to Sweden." Within a matter of minutes the Danish Navy ceased to exist: twenty-nine ships were scuttled; thirteen, mostly auxiliary small craft, were on their way to Sweden, where they were later interned; and six fell into German hands.[5]

The Danish Jews could not quite make up their minds about what attitude to take toward this beginning of organized resistance against the Germans. As one Jewish government official stated: "We were glad to see that the Danes were starting to take a definite position against our mortal enemies the Germans. We knew what the Germans were doing to the Jews in all of the other occupied countries. At the same time, we had been left completely alone by them here in Denmark. Many of us were fearful that any resistance actions by the Danes might cause the Germans to change their attitude and start reprisals against us, the Danish Jews."

The fears of these Danish Jews were not unfounded. Despite their anxiety, however, they took no steps to assure their own safety. After August 29, 1943, reprisals were a reality. Yet the Danish Jews preferred not to have to think about it. When they did think about it, they hoped that by some miracle their unfettered freedom would continue and they would escape the fate of their fellow Jews throughout the continent. But resistance and reprisals did at least one thing for the Danish Jews: it increased their awareness and sensitivity to

the oncoming crisis. When the rumor of the German raid
reached them on the eve of Rosh Hashana, they were ready
to believe it. More important, they were ready to act upon it.

As for Best, he was under pressure from two sides, from
Hitler and from the Danes. Hitler's desire to liquidate all Jews,
including Danish Jews, was forcing him to begin a series of
Aktionen against them; and the Danish resistance, which had
already cost Best his position of plenipotentiary, was becoming more active. To save face, he decided to act. On September 8, 1943, a little over a week after the Danish government
had resigned and the Danish Navy had scuttled itself, he sent
a telegram to Berlin suggesting that the present state of emergency afforded him the very opportunity he needed for the
arrest and deportation of the Danish Jews to German concentration camps. He stated that for the carrying out of his plans
he would need special contingents of Gestapo, German troops
and transport vessels, "so that the Jewish problem can be
handled during the present siege and not later."[6]

Hitler was so delighted with Best's telegram that he immediately reinstated him as plenipotentiary, and instructed Hannecken to take orders from Best. This reversal of the previous
decision greatly angered Hannecken. In addition, Hitler instructed Ribbentrop to see to it that all of Best's needs for the
coming operation were met. Ribbentrop assigned Reichs-
führer Himmler to the task. Several days later, Best received
the following telegram from Ribbentrop: "THE REICH FOR-
EIGN MINISTRY ASKS YOU TO PUT FORWARD CONCRETE PRO-
POSALS WITH REGARD TO THE DEPORTATION OF JEWS DECIDED
UPON, IN ORDER TO DETERMINE HOW MANY POLICEMEN AND
HOW MANY S.S. SHOULD BE DETAILED TO THE IMPLEMENTA-
TION OF THE OPERATION IN QUESTION."[7]

Best now knew that there could be no turning back. On
September 11, he sent the telegram listing his needs, and received word in reply that his requirements would be met and

the men directly in charge of the raid would be Pancke and Mildner.

Best immediately set out to inform members of his own staff of the coming operation. The first one he contacted was his head of shipping operations, Georg Ferdinand Duckwitz.

Chapter 4 CONSCIENCE

> *The missionaries of Christianity had said in effect:*
> *You have no right to live among us as Jews. The*
> *secular rulers who followed had proclaimed: You*
> *have no right to live among us. The German Nazis*
> *at last decreed: You have no right to live.*
>
> —RAUL HILBERG,
> *The Destruction of*
> *the European Jews*

DUCKWITZ HAD COME to Denmark from Germany in 1928, when, upon graduation from law school, he had obtained a position with a German coffee firm in Copenhagen. After the German invasion of Denmark, he had been given a post in the German Embassy as head of shipping in Copenhagen. Over the years he and his wife had made many friends among the Danes, including the heads of the Danish Social Democrat Party.[1]

His first inkling of German plans to arrest Danish Jews came on September 11, 1943, when Best informed him of pressure that was being put upon him by Hitler himself to do something about the Jews in Denmark. Ribbentrop had requested Best to submit plans and needs for an operation destined to deport all Danish Jews to German concentration camps. Duckwitz told Best that he would be ashamed of being a member of the German Embassy staff if Best participated in Jewish persecution. Best replied that he was personally unsympathetic to the Nazis' treatment of the Jews, but claimed that it was necessary to obey orders. A heated argument ensued between the two men, during which Duckwitz walked out on Best and returned to his home.

Several hours later Duckwitz received a telephone call from Best requesting his presence at the Embassy. When he arrived, an embarrassed Best confessed that their argument that afternoon had been purely academic. Earlier in the day he had sent a telegram to Berlin outlining his plan for the arrest of the Danish Jews.

"Why do you tell me this now?" asked Duckwitz.

"Perhaps," replied Best weakly, "the plan will be turned down as impractical."

On September 13, Duckwitz flew to Berlin from Copenhagen and prudently inquired at the Foreign Ministry about Best's telegram. He was informed that Ribbentrop had passed the telegram on to Hitler, who had given it his approval and had instructed Himmler to solve all the technical questions involved in the arrest and transport of the Danish Jews to Theresienstadt Concentration Camp. Best was to receive whatever troops, trucks and transport ships he thought necessary. Duckwitz returned to Copenhagen that evening with no idea of how he could possibly help the Danish Jews, but determined to keep carefully abreast of all developments.

On September 17, 1943, Danish Foreign Minister Niels Svenningsen called upon Best with a complaint. Members of the Jewish Community Center had told him that their offices had been broken into by Germans in civilian clothes and records containing members' names and addresses stolen. Best readily admitted knowledge of the incident, but claimed it was only *"eine recht kleine Aktion,"* a very small action, involving a routine search for saboteurs, and had absolutely nothing to do with "the Jewish question."

After Svenningsen left the German Embassy, Best confided to Duckwitz that the seizure of the records was indeed the necessary preparation of a planned raid. Asked when the raid would take place, Best told Duckwitz that he would be kept informed, especially since, as head of shipping, he would be involved in the operation. The following day Best told him that on September 29 several German transport ships would anchor in the harbor of Copenhagen in preparation for transporting to Germany the eight thousand Jews who would be arrested during a carefully planned "lightning raid" on October 1.

On September 18, a special group of S.S. commandos arrived in Copenhagen, sent by the department of Adolf Eichmann. In charge was Eichmann's second in command, S.S. Major Rolf Guenther, who was later to distinguish himself by his effective use of Zyklon B poison gas in the death camps.

Best had acted, and his actions so pleased Hitler that the Führer now appointed him virtual dictator of Denmark. But he was still a man beset by doubts. He knew that from all indications arrest and deportation of the Danish Jews would encourage the Danish population to greatly increased resistance activity, but he had no way of gauging to how great an extent. Furthermore, his chief of transport was opposed to the plans for the raid on moral grounds and, in addition, the army commander of the operation, Hannecken, bore a personal grudge against him. Even the Gestapo officer in charge of the raid, Mildner, opposed the operation out of fear of Danish repercussions. Nevertheless, Best had to finish what he had started, and plans for the roundup proceeded according to schedule.

On September 23, Best encountered the difficulties he had anticipated with Hannecken. The General informed Best that despite the presence of Guenther and his Eichmann commandos, he had written to General Wilhelm Keitel, chief of the Wehrmacht High Command, in Berlin, requesting that the deportations take place *after* the military emergency in Denmark was over. "The implementation of the Jewish deportations," he had written, "impairs the prestige of the Wehrmacht."[2] He claimed that during the present emergency, despite the fact that Best had been reinstated as plenipotentiary, it was still the Wehrmacht that was responsible for maintaining order, and he could not guarantee order if the Gestapo was permitted to carry out the raid. He had further warned that the raid would be unpopular enough among the Danes to result in the possible "loss of Danish meat and fats."

Best wondered how Berlin would take to Hannecken's recommendation. The following day the letter came back to Copenhagen with a message scrawled on it by General Alfred Jodl: "Nonsense. These are matters of state necessity." Nothing could now stand in the way of the raid. Best suggested that a system for rounding up the Jews that had been extremely successful in some of the other occupied countries be employed in Denmark. This was the issuing of an edict ordering the Jews to report for "work" to the Wehrmacht offices. Upon arrival, they would be arrested and deported. Eichmann's commandos rejected this proposal, preferring a lightning raid on Jewish homes in the middle of the night.

On September 25, 1943, knowing full well the consequences if caught, Duckwitz, on his own initiative, flew from Copenhagen to Stockholm, where he asked Swedish diplomat Ekblad to arrange for him to meet with the prime minister, Per Albin Hansson. Late that Sunday morning, a secret meeting was arranged between the two at Hansson's apartment. Duckwitz told Hansson of the danger facing the Danish Jews and insisted that the Swedish government tell the German government that Sweden would be willing to accept all of

Denmark's eight thousand Jews. Hansson replied that he could not answer immediately for the Swedish government, but agreed to convene an emergency meeting of the Swedish cabinet and to inform him of its decision. Later that evening he again met with Duckwitz at the apartment to tell him that Sweden would accept the Jewish refugees providing Germany approved.

"The telegram has already been sent to Berlin," said Hansson. "Our Embassy in Copenhagen will inform you of Berlin's reply." Duckwitz flew back to Copenhagen.

Two days passed during which Duckwitz received no word from the Swedish Embassy. On Thursday evening, September 29, Duckwitz assumed correctly that the Germans had decided to ignore the telegram from Sweden. He knew that the Danish Social Democrats were having a meeting that very evening. In a little over twenty-four hours the raid would take place. Telling his wife that he would be back within the hour, Duckwitz left his apartment and walked to 22 Roemer Street, where the Social Democrats were convening. Entering the main meeting room of the building, he approached Hans Hedtoft, head of the Social Democrat Party. Hedtoft recalled him as being "white with indignation and shame."

"The disaster is here," Duckwitz said. "Everything is planned in detail. In a few hours ships will anchor in the harbor of Copenhagen. Those of your poor Jewish countrymen who get caught will forcibly be brought on board the ships and transported to an unknown fate."

Hedtoft barely had time to say "Thank you" before Duckwitz disappeared.

Hedtoft quickly told H. C. Hansen and the other leaders of the Social Democrat Party the information Duckwitz had just given him, and it was decided to inform C. B. Henriques, the head of the Jewish community, as quickly as possible.

When Hedtoft arrived at Henriques' home, he wasted no time in getting to the point.

"Mr. Henriques," said Hedtoft, "the thing we have feared so long has come into being. Tomorrow night the Gestapo will raid all Jewish homes to arrest the Jews and bring them to boats in the harbor. Being head of the Jewish community, you must warn everybody. Of course, we'll assist you in every way we can."

Henriques' reaction was quite different from what Hedtoft had expected. He said only two words: "You're lying."

As Hedtoft desperately went on talking, trying to convince him of the seriousness of the situation, Henriques suddenly asked: "Where does your knowledge come from?"

Hedtoft, thinking it best not to mention Duckwitz' name, replied that it was from an authoritative source.

"I know you're wrong," said Henriques, "because I've just spoken to Foreign Minister Svenningsen, and he told me that Best assured him nothing would happen. Do you think Svenningsen would try to fool me?"

"Of course not," said Hedtoft. "Svenningsen said what he did in good faith. But he's only repeating what the Germans told him, what they want him to believe."

It was no use. Henriques was intransigent in his disbelief. Hedtoft left feeling that he had failed completely in his mission.

Returning to the meeting place of the Social Democrats, Hedtoft reported his unsuccessful meeting with Henriques to his friends. They decided to take it upon themselves to warn as many Jews as they could.

One of the men at the Social Democrats' meeting was Alsing Andersen. His secretary, Inge Barfeldt, was married to a German Jewish refugee living in Denmark. Andersen telephoned her to get the word to her husband, but Inge's husband was not at home. He was in the country receiving agricultural training as a *chaluz*, a potential agricultural set-

tler in Palestine. Inge immediately telephoned one of the organizers of the *chaluzim* in Denmark, Julius Margolinsky, a
librarian.[3]

"I must see you immediately," she said.

"What's wrong?" asked Margolinsky.

"I can't tell you over the telephone. Can I come over to
see you now?"

It was getting close to curfew time, but Margolinsky knew
from the tone of her voice that it was important.

"All right."

Within a few minutes Inge arrived and told Margolinsky
what she had heard. Margolinsky telephoned his good friend
Marcus Melchior, rabbi of the Copenhagen Synagogue.

"I am sending someone to see you with an important
message."

Several minutes later, Inge was telling the story to Rabbi
Melchior.

Melchior had in the past heard rumors of a possible mass
arrest of the Danish Jews, but he had discounted the rumors
as groundless. This time he knew that what the young girl
was telling him was founded in fact. The state of military
emergency, the stealing of the membership lists from the
Jewish Community Center, all led to an inescapable conclusion: this time the Germans meant business.

Tomorrow was the day before Rosh Hashana, and Melchior
knew that more than the usual number of worshipers would
be present in the synagogue. He decided to warn them of the
impending danger and to advise them to go into hiding at
once.

Chapter 5 THE WARNING

Where there is a heart, there is a house.

—Danish Proverb

Rabbi Melchior's warning to his congregation of the planned German raid stunned them into silence.[1] When he exhorted them to leave immediately to spread the word throughout Copenhagen, a few were too shocked to move.

"You must do what I tell you!" Melchior shouted, and those who had lingered behind departed, leaving the Rabbi alone in the deserted prayer hall.

Melchior was forty-six years old. He and his wife had five children. He wondered whom he could call upon to give refuge to his large family. He wondered about the holy objects of the synagogue—the scrolls of the Torah, silver candelabra, prayer books—where could they be safely hidden? He decided to call his friend Pastor Hans Kildeby, Lutheran minister at the Church of Ørslev, sixty miles south of Copenhagen. Pastor Kildeby told Rabbi Melchior to set out with his family for Ørslev as soon as possible.

"Perhaps I better come with only one or two of the children," said Melchior. "I'll find someplace else to hide the others."

"No," insisted Pastor Kildeby, "you must come with your entire family. We have plenty of space. I can put three rooms at your disposal."

"Are you sure you want us to come?" asked Melchior. "If you are caught hiding us, you may go to prison."

"I am ready to go to prison," replied Pastor Kildeby.

Before leaving with his family for Ørslev, Melchior contacted another Lutheran minister he knew—the pastor of the church down the street from the Copenhagen Synagogue. The Pastor agreed to hide all of the synagogue's holy objects in the cellar of his church.

Word of the planned German raid spread quickly. Following Melchior's instructions, those who had attended the early morning service at the synagogue pointed out to everyone they knew the importance of going into hiding. Some used the telephone, but most, fearing the lines might be tapped, preferred to deliver the warning in person. Jews told not only other Jews, but Christians whom they knew they could trust. Throughout the day, Christian policemen, postmen, taxi drivers, shopkeepers, doctors, teachers and students took time off from their work to give the warning to their Jewish friends and acquaintances. Students ran through the streets, entered cafés and restaurants, searching for Jews to warn.

Jørgen Knudsen, a young newly married ambulance driver, was leaving his apartment to report for work when he noticed some of his student friends rushing up and down the street stopping people. When he asked them what they were doing and they informed him, he exploded: "So the bastards have finally decided to do it! God damn them!"[2]

"Warn all your Jewish friends," said one of the students.

Knudsen had never thought in terms of Jewish or non-Jewish friends. Friends were friends. Names might be an indication, but for the moment he couldn't think of a single friend with a Jewish-sounding name.

He had to do something. On the street corner was a tele-

phone booth. He entered it and ripped out the telephone
directory. Hiding it under his coat, he walked rapidly to the
garage where his ambulance was parked. Sitting behind the
wheel of the ambulance, he opened the directory, and with a
pencil circled what were obviously Jewish names. He did not
report with his ambulance for hospital duty that day. Instead,
he drove throughout Copenhagen calling on total strangers to
give them the warning. When people he called upon became
frantic because they had no one to turn to, he piled them
into his ambulance and drove them to Bispebjerg Hospital,
where he knew Dr. Karl Henry Køster would be willing to
hide them.

Knudsen's spontaneous action was typical of the behavior
of a large segment of the Danes. When questioned later as to
why he acted the way he did, Knudsen matter-of-factly replied, "What else could I do?"—a statement of refreshing
contrast to what was said by so many Germans and other
nationals who, when asked why they never lifted a finger to
aid the Jews, replied, "What could I do?"

Another nonpolitical Dane who acted immediately, spontaneously, almost involuntarily, was Professor Richard Ege,[3]
head of the Biochemistry Research Division of the Rockefeller Institute in Copenhagen. He was in his laboratory when
an associate, Dr. Poul Astrup, entered and excitedly broke the
news to him.

"I know you have some Jewish friends," said Dr. Astrup.
"You must tell them to leave their apartments and go into
hiding in the homes of Christian friends."

Professor Ege knew that Dr. Astrup was a member of the
illegal Communist Party and engaged in underground activities. He undoubtedly had access to fact rather than rumor,
and Professor Ege decided to act upon his advice. Wary
about using the telephone, he thought it would be safest to
call personally on his Jewish friends. He exchanged his
laboratory smock for his coat, and left the Institute to begin

his rounds of calling at offices and homes. Some of the visits took longer than others, for many of his friends refused to believe at first that the raid was imminent, and it took time and a good deal of persuasion on Professor Ege's part to convince them. Others believed it immediately. Whenever any of his friends expressed the slightest concern about where they might be able to go into hiding, Professor Ege automatically suggested they move into his spacious apartment above the laboratory at the Rockefeller Institute.

Later that afternoon Professor Ege returned to his apartment and informed his wife of the news he had received earlier from Dr. Astrup and that they would be receiving "guests" later that evening. Mrs. Ege began contacting her Jewish friends. There was one among them whom she felt free to telephone—Mrs. Annemarie Glanner, a lifelong friend with whom, as a young girl, she had spent several years in Siam. Mrs. Ege was able to give her the warning over the telephone in Siamese.

Knudsen and Professor Ege and his wife acted out of non-political, purely humanitarian motivation. Ege warned the Jews because "it was a natural reaction to want to help good friends." His wife helped because "it was exactly the same as seeing your neighbor's house on fire. Naturally you want to try to do something about it."

Others, such as Jens Lillelund, a cash-register salesman, and Mogens Staffeldt, a bookshop owner, warned the Jews not only because it was the decent thing to do, but out of firm political conviction. Both men had been members of the Danish underground from the very beginning of the occupation, and warning Jews was an additional action in their general pattern of resistance activity.

Tall, lanky, balding Lillelund had taken his first action against the Germans the day they crossed into Denmark. Standing on a street corner in Copenhagen on the morning of April 9, 1940, he spat into the face of the first German soldier passing by. He was immediately seized by several German soldiers and thrown into a Danish prison. After being locked in a cell for several hours, he was brought before a Danish police officer who said, "I'm going to let you go this time. That is, I'm going to let you escape. There will be no guard at the back door. However, I want you to know that I think what you did was damned foolish and stupid." Lillelund couldn't help but agree with the police officer. He vowed that the next time he was arrested by the Germans it would be for something more significant, less foolish and stupid, than merely spitting in the face of one of them. From that first day of the occupation, Lillelund carried on a one-man campaign against the Germans by wandering on the streets at night and slashing the tires of their automobiles. Later he became a full-time saboteur, blowing up Danish factories in production for the Germans. When, on the morning of September 30, 1943, an underground contact informed him of the planned German raid, the first person he went to warn was his family physician, Dr. Max Rosenthal.

Dr. Rosenthal, in the midst of examining a patient, was startled to see Lillelund walk into his office.

"What's the matter with you, Lillelund?" snapped Dr. Rosenthal. "You know better than to come in here like this."

"I want to see you," said Lillelund.

"But I'm examining a patient now. Besides, there are other patients ahead of you in the waiting room."

"I must see you immediately," insisted Lillelund.

"Is it an emergency?"

"Yes," said Lillelund, "it's very definitely an emergency."

Several minutes later, Dr. Rosenthal, his wife and children were accompanying Lillelund to his house, where they were to remain in hiding for the next few days.

To help spread the warning among as many Jews as possible, Lillelund contacted several associates in the underground, including Mogens Staffeldt. Like Lillelund, the short,

mild-mannered bookshop-owner Mogens Staffeldt took his
first action against the Germans on April 9, 1940. Early that
morning he was awakened by a friend who informed him of
the German invasion and asked him whether he could help
some of the Polish Embassy staff out of the country. Staffeldt,
annoyed that his country had offered no resistance to the
Germans, agreed to help the Poles. He drove them in his car
from the Embassy to the north coast of Zealand, where they
were picked up by an English submarine. Later, when Staffeldt learned of Lillelund's underground activities, he volunteered his help. Staffeldt had moved at that time into a new
bookstore located in the building that housed the Gestapo
headquarters. At Lillelund's suggestion, Staffeldt allowed his
bookshop to become a secret headquarters for the underground and, in the cellar of the shop, began printing illegal
resistance newspapers containing accounts of German atrocities against the Jews of the other European countries. These
accounts were an important source of information for the
Danes on the brutal realities of Nazi ideology. When Staffeldt
received from Lillelund word of the planned roundup, he
immediately left for the shop of his friend, Bent Schottländer,
a furrier. Together they went to Schottländer's home, where
Staffeldt helped move Schottländer, his wife and three children to his own house. Returning to his store, Staffeldt told
his clerks he would be gone for the remainder of the day,
mounted his bicycle, and rode throughout Copenhagen to
pass the warning to over a dozen Jewish families. Among
those he warned was a shopkeeper, Emil Abrahamsen, who
dismissed as a silly rumor what Staffeldt had told him.
Abrahamsen was arrested the following day, and aboard the
German steamer taking him to Theresienstadt he committed
suicide by poison.

    In addition to Abrahamsen, there were others who received
the warning but did not believe it. When Carl Næsh Hendriksen, a crime reporter, heard the news, the first one he

telephoned was his friend Judge Moritz, who lived at Assens, a town eighty-four miles south of Copenhagen.

"Something is wrong," warned Hendriksen. "You must leave home right away with your sister. Do you know what I mean?"

"Yes, I know what you mean," replied the Judge. "You think the Germans are going to come after us. Now you listen to me. I'm not going anywhere. I'm a Dane. I live here. I'll stay here. The Germans wouldn't dare to do anything to us."

"But tomorrow night," said Hendriksen, "tomorrow night something important is—"

Moritz hung up on him.

The following evening Moritz was picked up by the Gestapo and shipped to Theresienstadt, where he died several weeks later.

Some people received the warning, and believed it, but did not want to act upon it. When Abram Krotoschinsky, a baker from Poland, received the warning, he lay down on his bed, turned his face to the wall and refused to move. His daughter Rosa, a dentist, tried to persuade him to leave the house.[4]

"It's no use," he said. "I'm tired of running. First it was Poland. Then Russia. Finally we settled here in Denmark. It's a wonderful country. The Danes are good to us. I don't want to leave. I'm too old to start all over again in another country, too old to run."

"But it will only be for a little while," pleaded Rosa.

Her father was adamant.

Finally she decided to try a new tack. As a half-Jew, Rosa had decided it would not be necessary for her or her mother, who was a Christian, to go into hiding. Her father, a full Jew, was the only one she had felt to be in danger. Now she told him that she had changed her mind and had decided that she, too, should hide from the Germans, and needed her father to accompany her. It was only on these grounds, for the sake of his daughter Rosa, that Abram Krotoschinsky decided once more "to run."

An eighty-four-year-old woman refused to go into hiding because she was certain that the Germans had better sense than to waste time on anyone her age. On the way to Theresienstadt she found among the other prisoners in her railroad cattlecar a woman who was 102 years old.[5]

Some received the warning and chose not to believe it, some believed it and chose not to do anything about it, but most believed it and acted upon it in a matter of minutes—or hours at the very most. Their ability to act quickly is important in understanding the success of their escape. Their willingness to act quickly is related to their knowledge that they had protectors in the Danish people.

The Danish Jews are to a large extent assimilated. The proportion of Jews married to Christians is probably higher in Denmark than in any country in the world. Most of the Danish Jews had close gentile relatives whom they knew they could call upon, and in those cases where there were no relatives, there were at least close friends. In those few cases where there were neither relatives nor close friends, there were acquaintances and even total strangers. One man helped by a total stranger was Mendel Katlev.[6]

Thirty-six-year-old Katlev was on the job as foreman of a leather-goods factory when he received a telephone call from his brother-in-law.

"You must come to my home immediately."

"What's wrong?" asked Katlev.

"I can't tell you over the phone."

"But it's impossible for me to walk off my job just like that."

"It's a matter of life and death."

"What is it?" demanded Katlev.

"I can't tell you over the telephone," repeated the brother-in-law.

Katlev was certain that his ailing father had taken a turn for the worse, and this is what he told his employer, who gave him permission to leave. As his brother-in-law's house was near the factory, he promised to return within the hour. He returned two years later.

His brother-in-law informed him of the impending raid, and Katlev decided to go home immediately. He had no idea of where he, his wife and two small sons could hide.

On the train to his house, his ticket was punched by the same conductor who usually punched it daily.

"How come you're going home so early today?" asked the conductor. "Are you sick? As a matter of fact, you don't look too well."

Katlev told him the news he had just learned.

"That's awful," said the train conductor. "What are you going to do?"

"I don't know," answered Katlev. "We'll have to find a place to hide."

"Come to my house," suggested the conductor. "Get your wife and your children and bring them all to my house."

"But you don't know me," said Katlev. "You don't even know my name, and I don't know yours."

"Carstensen," said the railroad conductor, holding out his hand.

"Katlev," said Katlev, shaking his hand.

While Katlev received help from a stranger, Magnus Ruben, a young orthodox Jew and a lawyer, was aided by an employee.[7]

Ruben had planned to leave his office early in the afternoon to help his wife prepare for the Rosh Hashana holidays. Just before departing, he decided to call his friend Erik Hertz to wish him a happy New Year.

"I'm afraid," said Hertz, "it won't be a very happy New Year for us."

"Why?"

"I'm not feeling well."

"Are you sick?"

"No, it's just that I'm not feeling well, my wife Ruth is not feeling well, my whole family is not feeling well, and you are not feeling well, too. I cannot say any more over the telephone. Do you understand?"

"I think so."

"We were supposed to receive guests this evening," said Hertz, "but we don't plan to be home. You shouldn't plan to be home, either."

Ruben turned to a twenty-two-year-old law student who was working in his office as an apprentice, and told him of the strange conversation he had just had with his friend Erik Hertz. They both agreed that it could mean only one thing— that the German raid they had heard rumors about was finally going to take place.

"You better stay with your wife at my room tonight," suggested the student.

"But you live in a students' dormitory where no girls are allowed."

"Don't worry about that," said the student. "We'll sneak her in."

"But if she should be discovered . . ."

"Let's not be concerned about breaking some old puritanical rules at a time like this," said the law student.

Ruben went home and found his wife washing dishes that had been left over from lunch. He told her why they had to leave immediately to meet the law student from his office.

"All right," said his young wife. "We'll leave as soon as I finish the dishes."

"There's no time to finish the dishes," said Ruben. "The Germans may be here any minute."

"But," asked Mrs. Ruben, "how will it look for them to find dirty dishes in the sink?"

Ruben had to employ force to get her to leave the dishes.

In 1943, as now, over 95 percent of the Jewish population of Denmark lived in Copenhagen. This geographical concentration greatly facilitated the dissemination of the warning. There had been no careful planning, no organization. The time had been too short. Word was spread as the result of an automatic mass response. People from all walks of life had reacted with conscience and a sense of personal responsibility. Thanks to the spontaneous, willing and effective cooperation of Jew and non-Jew, Rabbi Melchior's wish that within a matter of hours every Jew in Denmark know the danger that faced him was largely fulfilled. Word was gotten to almost everyone directly concerned, except the Germans.

When King Christian X learned of the German plans, he wrote a letter to Best and instructed Svenningsen to deliver it to him personally. After citing reports that the Germans "intend to take steps against the Jews of Denmark," the King added: "I desire to stress to you—not only because of human concern for the citizens of my country, but also because of the fear of further consequences in future relations between Germany and Denmark—that special measures in regard to a group of people who have enjoyed full rights of citizenship in Denmark for more than one hundred years would have the most severe consequences."[8]

The letter never reached Best, because he refused to see Svenningsen. He was too busy concluding his plans to bring the Final Solution to Denmark.

Shortly before midnight, September 29, 1943, two German transport vessels, including the large *Wartheland*, dropped anchor in Copenhagen Harbor.[9] Several hours later, after midnight, the Germans struck. Trucks filled with Gestapo commandos and special German police raced through the streets to arrest the eight thousand Jews living in Denmark. The Wehrmacht dispatched troops to cordon off Copenhagen Harbor in preparation for the embarkment of eight thousand Jews onto the transport vessels. A confident Werner Best prematurely sent the following telegram to Hitler: "IT WAS MY DUTY TO CLEAN DENMARK FROM HER JEWS, AND THIS IS ACHIEVED. DENMARK IS 'JUDENREIN'—CLEAN OF JEWS AND COMPLETELY PURGED."

Throughout the long night, the Gestapo, armed with address lists, raided the residences of Denmark's eight thousand Jews.

They were not at home.

With the exception of 202 Danish Jews who, for one reason or another, decided not to act upon the warning, mainly because they were too old or too ill to go into hiding, nobody was home. The roundup was a failure. It was to continue for several days, and the total number of Danish Jews captured and shipped to Theresienstadt was to rise to 472 by the end of October 1943.

But even on the morning of the first day of the raid it was obvious that the Germans had suffered the worst defeat in their entire operation to destroy world Jewry. When word of the failure reached Berlin, Hitler and Himmler, according to eyewitness accounts, "became raging mad with indignation."[10]

The arch Jew-killer of the German Reich was dispatched to Denmark to see if the situation could be corrected. Adolf Eichmann arrived on October 3.

He berated Best. He screamed at Mildner. All to no avail. The German transport vessel *Wartheland*, outfitted to hold thousands of prisoners, left Copenhagen Harbor with only 202 Danish Jews. The other transport vessel left empty.

Eichmann was forced to leave Denmark for more pressing business in eastern Europe. Before departing, he gave orders that the raids were to continue, that the Jews were to be found at all costs. It was impossible, he argued, for the Danish Jews to remain in hiding for more than a few days.

Chapter 6 **IN HIDING**

Invisible are the persecuted . . .

—Karl Roos

Saboteurs, illegal Communist Party mem-
bers, underground agents, all knew why they were in hiding.
They had taken it upon themselves to oppose the Germans,
and voluntarily faced the risks and consequences. But what
of the Danish Jew? He had not opposed the Germans. Why
was he in hiding? What was his crime? Nothing more than
that of millions of his European coreligionists. To be born
a Jew.

A saboteur faced a trial, possibly a jail sentence, probably
death. The Jew faced no trial, no jail sentence. He faced a
concentration camp and certain death, whether he was an old
man or a child. All that mattered was that he was a Jew.

The Danish Jew in hiding knew the fate met by all but a
handful of the Norwegian Jews who had remained in Norway after 1940.[1] He knew, too, the tragic events that had be-
fallen the Jews in all of the other German-occupied countries.
A rash of suicides broke out during those first days in hiding.
In Copenhagen, two sisters in their early twenties committed
suicide by throwing themselves under the wheels of a trolley
car. Several Jews hanged themselves, while others took gas.[2]

Many Jews, just before going into hiding, received from their physicians poison capsules which they planned to take if captured by the Germans. Several, believing the situation hopeless, convinced no one would really risk his life to help them, took the capsules before being caught.

There were Danes ready to risk their lives to help the Jews. There were many of them—as a matter of fact, almost the entire Danish population. When word reached the Jews of the actions of these fellow Danes, many of them became encouraged and hopeful. All suicides suddenly ceased.

The first step the Germans took to find the Jews in hiding was to announce that leading officers of the Danish Army and Navy, who had been arrested as hostages when the state of military emergency had been declared on August 29, 1943, would be released in exchange for information leading to the whereabouts of the Jews. Army General Goertz and Vice-Admiral Vedel rejected the offer and chose voluntary internment in prison. Goertz charged that release under these conditions would be degrading. Vedel, in replying to the Germans, said: "There is no point in exchanging one Dane for another Dane."[3]

Best felt that Goertz and Admiral Vedel, because of their exalted public positions as heads of the Danish armed forces, might take an idealistic stand, but hoped that Danish officers of lesser rank would welcome their freedom, and that the populace would surrender the Jews in hiding in grateful appreciation. On October 2, the Germans issued the following proclamation:

Since the Jews, who, with their anti-German provocation and their moral and material support to terrorism and sabotage, to a considerable extent contributed to the aggravated situation in Denmark, and since, thanks to the precautions taken by Germans, these Jews have been secluded from public life and prevented from poisoning the atmosphere, the German command will, in order to fulfill wishes cherished by most of the Danish people, begin to release within the next few days interned Danish soldiers, and this release will continue at a pace decided by the technical possibilities.

It didn't work. Neither did a second bribe—the lifting of the state of military emergency. Several officers accepted their release. The populace enjoyed the lifting of the restrictions of the military emergency, but no one, officer or civilian, with the rare exception of occasional informers, disclosed the hiding places of the Jews. On the contrary, the Danish people received encouragement from very important quarters to do everything possible to save the Jews in hiding from the Germans.

On October 2, the illegal newspaper *Free Denmark* appeared with a signed editorial by Christmas Møller, the Danish minister of trade. He wrote:

It is as if the Nazis' latest infamy, the persecution against the Jews, had destroyed the last, weak dikes which—strangely enough—in some places still stopped the stream of indignation . . . The persecution of the Jews has hit the Danes in the sorest point of their conception of justice; even the much too tolerant, the passive, the lukewarm can feel this meanness and shrink from it . . . People say they're surprised that the Germans really had the courage to do it. We cannot take part in this astonishment . . . from this power we expect no better than racial persecution. We know that this kind of brutality has been the Third Reich's specialty since 1933 . . . The Germans should not think that the sending home of soldiers or the formal annulment of the state of emergency will subdue the wave of indignation created by this infamy . . . We couldn't yield to the German threats when the Jews' well-being was at stake. Nor can we yield today, where hard punishment and the probability of being taken to Germany await us if we help our Jewish fellow countrymen. We have helped them, and we shall go on helping them by all the means at our disposal. The episodes of the past two nights have to us become a part of Denmark's fate, and if we desert the Jews in this hour of their misery, we desert our native country.

On October 3, the Danish Lutheran bishops sent a letter to German occupation officials in Denmark. In addition, it was read in every Lutheran church in the country. It stated:

We will never forget that the Lord Jesus Christ was born in Bethlehem of the Virgin Mary, according to God's promise to the Chosen People of Israel.

Persecution of the Jews conflicts with the humanitarian conception of the love of neighbors and the message which Christ's church set out to preach. Christ taught us that every man has a value in the eyes of God.

Persecution conflicts with the judicial conscience existing in the Danish people, inherited through centuries of Danish culture. All Danish citizens, according to the fundamental law, have the same right and responsibility under the law of religious freedom. We respect the right to religious freedom and to the performance of divine worship according to the dictates of conscience. Race or religion should never in themselves cause people to be deprived of their rights, freedom or property.

Notwithstanding our separate religious beliefs we will fight to preserve for our Jewish brothers and sisters the same freedom we ourselves value more than life. The leaders of the Danish Church clearly comprehend the duties of law-abiding citizens, but recognize at the same time that they are conscientiously bound to maintain the right and to protest every violation of justice. It is evident that in this case we are obeying God rather than man.

After Pastor Ivar Lange of Frederiksberg Church read the bishops' proclamation, he added a comment of his own. "Politics must not be discussed here, because it is punishable," he said. "In spite of this, I tell you that I would rather die with the Jews than live with the Nazis."

In every Lutheran church in Denmark the bishops' letter was followed by prayers for the safety of the Jews.

Dean Johannes Nordentoft, writing in a journal for Danish pastors, commented: "Christians will be the first to fight this dirty anti-Semitism." He also described as Nazi accomplices those who "remain silent or disapprove by merely shrugging their shoulders." Kaj Munk, Danish minister, poet and playwright, delivered a sermon in which he said: "When here in this country pogroms have been started against a special group of our fellow countrymen, only because they belong to a special race, then the church has a right to cry out. This is breaking the constitution of Christ's kingdom and is abominable to the Nordic way of thinking. The church must here be indefatigable."

Many Danes who had assiduously avoided doing anything that might offend the Germans reacted without hesitation when it came to hiding the Jews. One of these was Aage Bertelsen, the headmaster of a school at Lyngby. When Germany invaded Denmark, Bertelsen was teaching in a high school in Gävle, in northern Sweden. He was relieved to learn that his country had capitulated without fighting. He thought of his family in his semidetached house in Buddinge Lane, outside of Copenhagen, and was happy that he would be able to return to Denmark to find his family and home unharmed and his country undevastated. "In all essentials," Bertelsen later admitted, "I had been at first an adherent of the so-called collaboration policy."[4] Bertelsen returned to Denmark and, as the years of the occupation rolled by, he grew increasingly opposed to the Germans but, because of his pacifist convictions, he steadfastly refused to participate in any underground activities against them. However, news of the German raid against the Jews made him change his mind. He knew Hebrew, had written a book on the Old Testament and had good friends who were Jewish. When, on October 1, Mrs. Sven Norrild, a teacher's wife, asked Bertelsen if he would be willing to help hide the Jews, he agreed immediately to do everything he could to help them. The following day, sixty Danish Jews were in hiding in his school. "From now on," commented Bertelsen, "there was no doubt or uncertainty possible. In the face of these open acts of atrocity, insanely meaningless, it was not a question of one's viewpoint. Action was the word. Even under serious or desperate conditions it is often a happy feeling to be able to devote oneself to a cause that one feels convinced is both unconditionally just and absolutely binding. The situation in Denmark at that time was precisely that simple. No honest man could possibly refrain from action after this raid, when the persecuted cried for help."

Captain Christian Kisling and his wife Gethe were also among those who, despite ideological antipathy toward the Germans, conscientiously avoided getting involved in any actions against them. Like Bertelsen, they changed their minds once the Germans attempted the roundup of the Danish Jews. When Germany invaded Denmark, Kisling had been at sea near the British West Indies. He received word of the invasion from the wireless operator of his tanker, *Bente Maersk*, and his sole concern was for his wife and two small children back in Copenhagen. He rejoined them via Portugal, Italy and Germany, and was happy to find them well and his country unharmed. While he had no intention of opposing the German occupation forces, neither did he want to aid them, and so, instead of returning to sea, where he would have to sail for the Nazis, he took a job on dry land with a Danish salvage company. On September 30, 1943, the Kislings heard that the German raid on the Jews was to take place imminently, but they refused to believe it. That night they realized how wrong they had been. They were awakened by the screeching of trucks coming to a sudden halt outside their apartment house. A few seconds later they heard the ominous sound of jack boots on the back staircase which led to the apartment of their Jewish neighbors. The sound of the boots was followed by the pounding of a rifle butt against the door and by cries of "Open up!"

"And we didn't believe it!" said Captain Kisling.

There were a few moments of silence, followed, for the

second time, by the pounding of the rifle butt against the door. Then more silence.

"Maybe they're not home," said Mrs. Kisling. "Maybe they've gone into hiding."

Kisling and his wife got out of bed and listened at the door. The only sound they now heard was the heavy boots crashing down the stairs. Crossing to the window, they saw the S.S. leave the building empty-handed.

"Good!" exclaimed Mrs. Kisling. "No catch."

"We've got to do something," said Kisling. "Starting tomorrow."

Above the garage of the salvage company for which Kisling worked was a large empty attic. It was a perfect hiding place for the Jews and by the following night forty of them were hidden there. Friends of the Kislings contributed army cots, blankets and pillows. Feeding the refugees was a problem, not because of the ration cards or money involved (many of the refugees had brought their ration cards and some money with them), but because Mrs. Kisling did not want to arouse suspicions by suddenly buying huge quantities of foodstuffs at the stores where she usually shopped or by walking through the streets with ten loaves of bread. To avoid suspicion, she made normal-sized purchases at a variety of stores at different times of the day. She would prepare the sandwiches and coffee at home and stealthily send them over to the refugees at night after dark. Not knowing whether or not she could trust her maid, she insisted that she take her youngest child outdoors for long airings, regardless of the weather, while she attended to the work involved in preparing food for forty people. More important than satisfying the hunger of the refugees was assuaging their fears, and during the several days that the initial group of refugees was in hiding with the Kislings, the Captain and his wife got very little sleep. Most of the evening hours were spent sitting up talking to the refugees, trying to keep their spirits up and maintaining a vigil on those among them who looked desperate enough to try to take their own lives.

"Those were indeed horrible days for all of us," Mrs. Kisling later commented. "It was not easy to enjoy one's own warm bed at night, knowing your countrymen were frightened and uncertain about what was going to happen to them, not knowing where to escape, where to turn."[5]

The Jews were in hiding everywhere—in the homes of Christian relatives, friends, total strangers, in Protestant churches and Catholic cloisters, in hotels, summer huts, cellars, warehouses, on farms and in hospitals. No group was more helpful than the physicians. When word of the German raid reached the hospitals, in a matter of minutes Danish Jews with Jewish-sounding names were "discharged" and "readmitted" with false, Christian-sounding names.[6] Several hundred Jews had fled in panic to the woods outside Copenhagen. Hundreds of Danish students organized searching parties to search the woods for them in order to bring them to safer hiding places. Large estate owners opened their homes to these refugees after they had been found by the students.

Hiding a single person, or even a couple, presented relatively few difficulties. However, where larger families were concerned problems arose. Not only was it often difficult to find space for these larger families, but there was the tragedy inherent in the possible capture of an entire family. For this reason, even if enough space could be found in a single residence to house an entire large family, it was often thought best to distribute the members of the family among several Christian homes, on the chance that should there be a raid on one home, relatives hidden elsewhere might escape. Despite the practical wisdom of this plan, there was often anxiety and heartbreak when a family was divided. Mothers, fathers, sisters and brothers wondered if they would ever see each other again.

The Jews were in hiding, but could not remain so indefinitely. The Germans were redoubling their efforts to find them. Unless they could be transported out of the country to neutral territory within a matter of days, they were bound to be detected.

The most obvious haven for them was several miles across the sound in neutral Sweden. But there was the question of whether Sweden would accept the Jewish refugees. And even if Sweden agreed to accept them, there remained the problem of transporting them past the Gestapo, the few Danish Nazis and informers, and, most dangerous of all, the German naval patrol.

Within the past month Sweden had made two proposals to Germany. The first was an offer to intern all Danish Jews. The second was an appeal for Germany to allow Sweden to accept all Danish Jewish children. The first offer, which had come about as a result of Duckwitz' secret visit to Sweden, was ignored. The second offer, to save Danish Jewish children, was turned down by Germany in no uncertain terms. "It was not appreciated here," State Secretary Steengracht told the Swedish minister in Berlin, "why Sweden was unequivocably taking the side of Bolshevism, while our blood and the blood of our allies was being expended to keep the Communist danger from Europe and thus also from the Nordic countries . . . If the occasion arose, this attitude would force us to answer in a manner not to be misunderstood."[7]

Here was clearly a German threat to Sweden's dearly prized neutrality. After such a threat, would Sweden dare to offend Germany by offering refuge to the Danish Jews? Certainly nothing in the past had indicated that Sweden would do anything to offend or intimidate Germany. Indeed, many observers had questioned Sweden's so-called neutrality as a blind for a decidedly pro-German attitude.

Was it neutrality to ship large quantities of arms to the Finns to fight the Russians, but refuse to send any arms, including ammunition and gasoline, to the Norwegians to fight the Germans?[8] Was it neutrality for the Swedish Foreign Ministry to allow the Germans to send naval messages in code through the Swedish minister in Buenos Aires directing German U-boat attacks on allied shipping? And what was neutral about allowing the Swedish State Railway, at a profit of $22,000,000, to transport hundreds of thousands of German troops and vast amounts of war material to garrisons in Norway—troops and war material which the British Navy might have sunk at sea, had Sweden refused land transport? What was neutral in supplying Germany with Swedish iron ore and ball bearings, without which the German war machine could not have functioned? In addition, it was well known how Swedish industry, some members of the royal family, the high-ranking Swedish army officers, government functionaries and several influential newspapers were pro-German. Would a country of such highly specious neutrality be willing to defy Germany and offer refuge to the Danish Jews?

Two factors augured a positive response. The first was that the time was October 1943, and it was becoming clear that the Allies would probably win the war. However, time was running out faster for the Danish Jews than for the Germans, and Sweden had to give her answer immediately. A delay of several days might very likely crush all hopes of possible rescue for the Danish Jews. The second factor was the arrival in Sweden on October 1 of one of the twentieth century's greatest geniuses, Nobel-Prize-winning physicist Niels Bohr.[9]

In 1943 there was only one man in the entire world who knew more about nuclear physics than Niels Bohr—his good friend Albert Einstein. The Allies very much wanted Bohr in the United States to work on the atom bomb. On September 30, Bohr was smuggled across the sound from Denmark to Sweden in a small boat. Upon arriving in Sweden, Bohr was greeted by Professor Frederick Lindemann, Churchill's personal consultant in scientific questions. Lindemann (later Lord

Cherwell) informed Bohr of the Allies' plan. He was to leave
immediately by plane for London, and then go to the United
States. Much to Lindemann's amazement, Bohr refused. He
said that he would not leave Sweden until an appointment
was arranged for him with the Swedish foreign minister. The
appointment was set for the following morning and Bohr left
directly for Stockholm.

Just before leaving Denmark, Bohr had been told by his
friend Hans Hedtoft about the German plans for rounding
up the Danish Jews. Meeting the Swedish foreign minister,
Bohr announced that he had no intention of leaving Sweden
until the foreign minister promised refuge to all Danish Jews
who were able to reach Swedish shores. Angered by the
Swedish foreign minister's uncooperative response, Bohr demanded an audience with the Swedish king. King Gustav
assured Bohr that he was sympathetic to the problem and
would give it his careful consideration. The next day Bohr
received word from King Gustav that Sweden would accept
the Danish Jews.

Allied agents in Stockholm breathed a sigh of relief. They
assumed that Bohr would now be willing to leave for London,
but they were wrong. What good was King Gustav's assurance, argued Bohr, if the Danish Jews did not know about it?
The Allies were anxious to get Bohr to America and fearful
of his being kidnaped or killed by German agents in Stockholm, but Bohr refused to leave the country until Sweden's
assurance to the Danish Jews was announced on the front
pages of Sweden's leading newspapers and broadcast over the
radio to Denmark. Bohr's demands were conveyed to King
Gustav, and several days later exactly what Bohr wanted
occurred. The Swedish press carried the offer of refuge on
its front pages and the government-owned Swedish radio
beamed the message to Denmark. After the broadcast, Bohr
left for London in the bomb bay of an unarmed R.A.F.
"Mosquito." Because of a faulty oxygen mask, Bohr arrived

in London unconscious, but he was not seriously hurt. Before continuing on to the United States, Bohr met in London with the king of Norway. King Haakon's joy over Bohr's success in Sweden was saddened only by his bitter recollection to Bohr of the fact that Sweden had made no such offer in regard to the Norwegian Jews, many of whom, as a consequence, had been killed by the Germans.

When word of the Swedish offer reached Denmark, protected and protector, Danish Jew and Danish non-Jew, were delighted. Only the Germans were furious.

One question remained—how to get to Sweden.

ILLUSTRATIONS

An anti-Nazi cartoon from the Danish humor magazine *Aandehullet*
("Breathing Hole"), closed down in 1934 after the German government protested. The caption is a parody on a speech of *Propagandamin-
ster* Josef Goebbels. "... High stature, blond hair, blue eyes, oval-shaped
face and a small nose is what characterizes the true, the pure Aryan...."

Another anti-Nazi cartoon from *Aandehullet*. The caption read: "The Nazis have announced that they will 'revenge themselves by a reign of terror which will be talked about 1000 years hence.' When Kuerten, the horrible mass-murderer of Düsseldorf has been forgotten, the name of HITLER will still live."

Saturday, October 2, 1943. One of the rare successful German raids on a Jewish household. Two Jews were taken; one resisted and was shot—hence the ambulance, at the left, in front of the Gestapo truck.

A fishing vessel, loaded to the gunwales with refugees, approaches neutral Sweden.

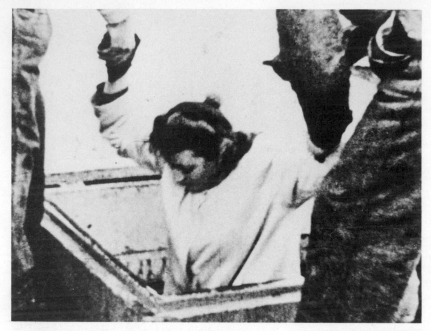

A refugee is lifted from the fishing hold of a boat after a successful escape.

Jewish refugees on the deck of a fishing boat.

A Jew has just been discovered by a Danish Nazi (center, in black rain-
coat and hat). An angry crowd is forcing him to hand the prisoner over
to the Danish police, who later helped him to escape.

Ole Lippman, who worked closely with Staffeldt and Truelsen.

Mogens Staffeldt (right), with his friend Sven Truelsen, a lawyer. Together the two men led an underground movement from Staffeldt's bookshop.

Erik Staermose, one of the heads of the Danish-Swedish Refugee Service.

Ole Helwig, who worked with Erik Staermose to save 750 Jews.

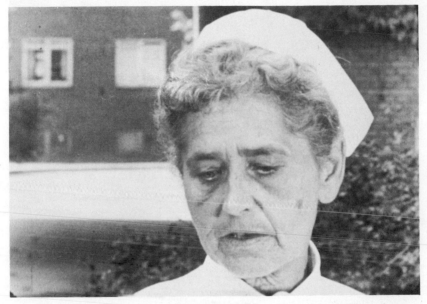

Head Nurse Signe Jansen of the Bispebjerg Hospital in Copenhagen, who was instrumental in finding hiding places for the 2000 Jews who passed secretly through the hospital on their way to Sweden.

Chief Rabbi Friediger and other Jews returning to Denmark from
Theriesenstadt concentration camp after the war.

Part Three

THE EXODUS

Chapter 7 FLIGHT

Then steal away, give little warning,
Choose thine own time;
Say not "Good night," but in some brighter clime
Bid me "Good morning."
— ANNA LETITIA BARBAULD

THERE WAS ONLY ONE WAY for the Danish Jews to get to Sweden—by boat. However, several days before the raid of October 1 the Germans had ordered that all Danish boats be taken out of the water and brought at least 1,000 feet inland. There was only one exception to this order—the fishing boats.

Immediately after Sweden's publicly announced offer of refuge to the Danish Jews, several hundred of them in hiding made a beeline to the coastal towns where they hoped to find fishermen who would be willing to ferry them across the sound to Sweden. While most of the Danish Jews were fearful of coming out of hiding to attempt to reach the coastal towns, these several hundred piled into taxicabs and headed for Elsinore, Snekkersten, Stevns and Dragør. A high official in the Danish foreign ministry, active at the time in the Socialist Youth Movement, reported the flight.[1] "It was interesting to see

on the road at the time many taxis loaded with Jews headed
for the seacoast towns. In many cases the taxi drivers were well
paid for their services, but, still, they were taking an awful
chance, for it was illegal to help the Jews to escape. I've heard
it said that some Germans, particularly members of the
Wehrmacht as opposed to the Gestapo, looked aside, closed
one eye, and let the Jews escape, but I don't believe this to be
true. Rather, it all happened so fast that they were taken by
surprise and fooled. They became quite angry, and, as a matter
of fact, did everything they could to stop the refugees."

Snekkersten and Elsinore, where the sound separating Denmark from Sweden is only two and a half miles wide, received
the majority of these refugees. The local inhabitants cooperated
in putting them up in hotels, inns, farms, garages and private
homes. Werner Christiansen, owner of a coastal resort inn at
Rødvig, turned his entire establishment over to them, and
placed the overflow with local townspeople and farmers. Not
one of the scores of local inhabitants he approached turned him
down when he asked them to hide the Jews.

The flight to the coastal towns during these first days of
October was disorganized and chaotic. The majority of the 472
Danish Jews caught by the Germans were captured during this
time.

The absent-minded Jewish editor of the Danish newspaper
Politiken was arrested during this period.[2] When stopped on
the street after curfew by German soldiers who asked him what
he was doing carrying a valise, he replied, "I'm fleeing."

"What do you mean?" asked one of the soldiers.

"You see," said the editor, "I'm Jewish and Sweden has said
she will accept all Danish Jews. So I'm fleeing to Snekkersten."

During this first week in October, a short, fifty-year-old
tailor showed up at the house of one of his customers, Stig
Hansen, a civil engineer.[3] Hansen was shocked to see him.

"My God, what are you doing here? Haven't you heard . . ."

"Yes, yes," interrupted the tailor, "I've heard all about it. You owe me money."

"Are you crazy?" asked Hansen. "You should be in hiding!"

"I can't afford it. I've heard Sweden is going to take us in if we can get there and I need some money for the fare. The only way we can get there is by fishing boats, and the fishermen will probably charge an arm and a leg."

"I'll lend you the money," said Hansen.

The tailor raised his chin proudly. "I have made it a lifelong principle never to borrow money."

"But this is an exceptional circumstance," said Hansen. "You can pay me back when this mess is over."

"No, no," said the tailor. "I'll go around to all the customers who owe me money, and if all of them pay me what they owe me, perhaps then my wife and I will be able to afford to go."

"You'll never make it that way," protested Hansen. "You'll be picked up by the Gestapo. Take the money from me."

The tailor hesitated. "I never borrow money," he repeated.

Hansen paid him what he owed him. The tailor stood holding the money in one hand, scratching his head with the other.

"Yes?" asked Hansen. "What are you thinking about?"

"My wife has a fur coat," said the tailor. "Does your wife need a fur coat? I could sell it to you cheap."

Hansen accompanied the tailor to his house. He and his wife lived rather poorly. It was obvious to Hansen that he earned barely enough to make ends meet, and if there was any profit it was undoubtedly spent on the large collection of books scattered about the house. The fur coat he showed Hansen was moth-eaten. Nevertheless, Hansen offered him the equivalent of seventy-five dollars for it. He looked around the apartment. The furniture was old and seedy.

"You know," said Hansen, "I could use some of these pieces of furniture. I don't want you to think I'm trying to take advantage of you, but how about selling me these two chairs for another seventy-five dollars?"

The tailor agreed.

"Now you have a hundred and fifty dollars," said Hansen. "That should be enough for the fare to Sweden."

"Yes," agreed the tailor, "but I don't know anyone to take us there."

Hansen took the tailor and his wife to the estate of his friend A. P. Møller, a shipbuilder in Hellerup. Møller promised to see to it that somehow or other the tailor and his wife would get to Sweden.

It was also during this period of haphazard attempts to flee to the coastal towns that several of the fishermen contacted to take the Jews across to Sweden charged exorbitant fees.[4] It cannot be denied that in making the trip they were risking not only their boats but their very lives. However, this was still no excuse for those instances where mercenary fishermen milked the desperate refugees for every cent they could. During the first week of October, some fishermen demanded and received as much as five thousand dollars per passenger. It must be pointed out that the charging of exorbitant rates was confined only to relatively few fishermen. Later on, the average crossing cost sixty dollars per passenger. Also, there were many fishermen who took the refugees across for nothing. There is not a single case on record of a refugee failing to reach Sweden because he lacked the fare, and many of the refugees had no money to pay. For every fisherman who overcharged the Jews, there were a dozen who ferried them across out of a genuine desire to be of help.

Peder Christopher Hansen[5] was among those who did it out of idealism. His actions in transporting Danish Jews and resistance people to Sweden earned him honors and citations from the American as well as Danish governments. His first brush with the Germans occurred at 7 A.M. on April 9, 1940. Hansen was returning to port with 5,000 kilos of cod in the hold of his boat, when he was stopped by an armed German trawler. Four German soldiers hopped on board.

"We want some fish," said one of the Germans.

"What the hell do you mean you want some fish! Are you pirates?"

"No," replied the soldier, "we'll pay for it."

"Even if you're willing to pay, you krauts have no right to be here. These are Danish territorial waters."

"Haven't you heard?" asked the soldier, laughing. "We're at war with you!"

At that moment, German planes appeared overhead. "Those are our bombers," said the soldier. "They're on their way to Copenhagen."

"They will be shot down," said Hansen.

"No, they won't," replied the soldier.

"If we're at war, they'll be shot down."

"No, they won't," insisted the soldier. "It isn't much of a war you Danes are fighting. There have been a few shots at the frontier, but that's all. In Copenhagen the government has already capitulated."

The Germans paid Hansen for the fish they took, and departed. Hansen was so disgusted with the fact that the Danes had not fought back that he changed the course of his boat and headed for Sweden. The heavy ice floes forced him to return, but did not cool him off.

During the first week of October 1943, Hansen was tying up his boat in the harbor of Rødvig, when he was approached by a sixty-year-old stranger.

"Can I speak to you in confidence?" whispered the man.

"What is it?" asked Hansen.

"I have to get my two sons to Sweden. We're Jewish and the Germans have started arresting all Danish Jews. Could you take them to Sweden? I'm willing to stay here and take a chance, but I must get my sons over."

"Yes," said Hansen. "I can take them. And I can take you, too."

"There are quite a few of us hiding here," said the man. "About how many others can you take?"

"How many are you?" asked Hansen.

"There are about fifty others hiding with my sons," said the man.

"I'll take them all," said Hansen. "I'll have to make more than one trip, but I'll take them all."

"Wonderful," said the man. "And don't worry. We're prepared to pay you for it."

"I don't give a damn about the money," said Hansen.

That night, Hansen made two trips to Sweden to get the fifty refugees across. It was his first illegal action against the Germans.

Two days later, a fisherman friend approached Hansen, saying, "Look, you have a daughter, so I know you can appreciate my situation. There are two young Jewish girls staying with me. Their parents have disappeared. Would you take them over to Sweden?"

"Yes," replied Hansen.

"They have no money."

"I don't care," said Hansen. "Anything I can do against the Germans is fine with me."

"Have you room for some other refugees in addition to the two girls? My own boat is full."

"Sure," said Hansen.

That night, at 1 A.M., Hansen led the two young girls and eight other Jewish refugees into the hold of his ship. Just as he was about to pull out, a spotlight hit the deck, and he was told to stand by. Ten German sailors boarded his ship.

"What are you doing at this hour of the night?" demanded the petty officer in charge.

"What does it look like I'm doing?" asked Hansen. "I'm setting out to fish. Now get the hell off my ship."

The German sailors were standing on top of the hold directly under which were hidden the ten Jewish refugees.

"I have the feeling," said the petty officer, "that you're involved in something else. I think we ought to search the ship."

Hansen decided to take a wild chance.

"You do that," he screamed, "and they'll hear about it at the German Naval Station at Korsør! What have you sons of bitches come to Denmark for? You're supposed to be here to protect us, not to bother us. Now get the hell off my ship or I'll sail with you on board right over to your commanding officer at Korsør, who happens to be a personal friend of mine, and I'll tell him what a hard time you've been giving me!"

The Germans left the ship and Hansen took the refugees over to Trelleborg in Sweden.

A week later, Hansen was contacted by resort-owner Werner Christiansen.

"I hear you've been taking Jewish refugees over to Sweden," said Christiansen.

"I've made a couple of trips," replied Hansen.

"Would you like to take some more over?"

"How many?"

"Four hundred."

"Four hundred!" exclaimed Hansen. "How big do you think my boat is?"

"And after you get those four hundred over, there may be others."

"What about my codfish?" asked Hansen. "Oh, hell, human beings are more important than codfish. Okay, I'll do whatever I can."

Another fisherman who acted out of idealism and was extremely active during the first week of flight was Axel Olsen.[6] He and his wife hated the Germans from the very first day they set foot in Denmark. On April 9, 1940, Olsen was on his way by bicycle to the docks when he noticed German planes overhead dropping leaflets. It was by picking up and reading one of them that he learned of Denmark's surrender to Germany. He turned his bicycle around and rode home to his wife and five-year-old son. His wife was still in bed sleeping, and when he awakened her to tell her what happened, she said simply, "It's a lie. I don't believe it. We wouldn't let them come in just like that without putting up a struggle." He showed her the leaflet, and, after reading it, she jumped out of bed, went into her son's room, gathered up his toy boats which had been made in Germany, threw them into the kitchen stove and burned them.

Olsen harbored resentment against the Germans from that time on, but it wasn't until the first week of October 1943 that he had an opportunity to put his resentment into concrete action. During the early part of that week, Olsen dragged up in his fishing net, in addition to dozens of cod, a dead man. The body was badly bloated, having been in the water for several weeks, but from its clothes, Olsen could see that it was the body of a Danish fisherman. He pulled it up on the boat and brought it to shore. The German soldiers at the nearby police station examined the corpse, questioned Olsen superficially and for only a few minutes, and, apparently convinced that there was nothing more to the story than he told, released him. Outside the prison, Olsen expressed to an Austrian guard his relief and astonishment over the dispatch with which he had been released.

"I thought they'd hold me much longer," said Olsen. "And I thought they'd give me a much harder time. After all, it's not every day that a fisherman brings up in his net a dead body."

"You're lucky," said the Austrian guard, "that they don't have time to bother with you today. They're all involved because of the failure of the raids during the past two nights."

"What raids?" asked Olsen.

"To arrest the Danish Jews," said the Austrian soldier. "From what I hear, they hardly caught any at all. They were all in hiding. Now they're trying to find out *where* they're hiding."

Walking toward his boat from the prison, Olsen was wondering what he could do to help the Jews in hiding when he bumped into a young baker's apprentice he knew. He thought it odd to see the boy walking down the middle of the street in his white clothes and hat, his hands and arms covered white with flour.

"What are you doing here?" asked Olsen. "Shouldn't you be in the bakery?"

Suddenly the boy broke down and cried.

"What's the matter?" asked Olsen.

"Haven't you heard of the German raids against the Danish Jews during the past few nights?" asked the boy.

"I just learned about it," said Olsen. "But what has that to do with you?"

"I'm Jewish."

"I never knew it," said Olsen.

"Nobody around here knows it," said the boy. "That's why I didn't go into hiding like the rest. But now I'm scared the Germans will find out. Several of the Jews in the town are trying to get to Sweden, but I have no money. I don't make much as an apprentice. In fact, I have only ten kroner."

Olsen got the boy to stop crying, took him to his house, fed him, dressed him in fisherman's clothes and took him to his boat. He had him remain in hiding at the bottom of the boat until after dark, and then took him over to Sweden.

Several days later, after an arduous fishing trip, Olsen was resting on his living room couch when Erik Beck, a friend who was a criminal lawyer, entered and told him that he was hiding the local police commissioner, Aage Lothinga, who was Jewish. Did Olsen, wondered Beck, know a fisherman who might be willing to take Lothinga over to Sweden? Olsen agreed to do the job himself. From that day until the war's end, Olsen was involved in the illegal transport of refugees.

Among those who attempted the flight to Sweden during the first week of October were Rabbi Melchior and his family.[7]

The son of Reverend Hans Kildeby, pastor of the church of Ørslev, made arrangements with a young fisherman to take Rabbi Melchior and his family to Sweden. By 7 P.M., when the Melchiors started out, the night was pitch-black. They left from the island of Falster, south of Zealand, and the trip in the small boat was to take six hours. Twelve hours later they were still at sea. As dawn broke, land appeared ahead of them. Melchior recognized the town of Gedser, a Danish town not far from the German frontier. The young fisherman, who had been behaving strangely all evening, confessed that because he was afraid of running into German patrol boats, all he had done throughout the long night was to circle about and finally bring them back to the Danish shore at a point not far from the German border. Melchior angrily knocked down the young fisherman, and, although he had never before steered a boat, grabbed the rudder and managed to turn the boat around in the direction of Sweden. He held the boat on course for six hours until they were safe in Swedish waters.

Within a matter of days it became evident to the Danes that if the exodus of Danish Jews to Sweden was to be successful, capricious acts of individual daring had to be replaced by some form of organized action. At the beginning, there had been no planning, no organization. But the challenge of saving the lives of eight thousand countrymen gave the Danes an enormous impetus to band together to prove that if the will was there, the Germans could be thwarted in their plan to exterminate Denmark's Jewry.

Chapter 8   NO CUSTOMERS WANTED

Fortune favors the brave.

—TERENCE

UNTIL SEPTEMBER 12, 1943, Mogens Staffeldt's bookshop was located in Dagmarhus, the same building used by the Gestapo as its Copenhagen headquarters. On that date the Gestapo took possession of the entire building and Mogens Staffeldt was forced to find new quarters. He moved into a store across the street. It was in the empty back room of this new store that a group of underground men met during the first week of October. They included Staffeldt, his younger brother Jørgen, Jens Lillelund and Sven Truelsen, a lawyer. Their purpose was to try to figure out an organized way of smuggling Denmark's Jews to Sweden.[1] They knew that individual attempts to get over were too dangerous. About two hundred of the refugees had attempted it during the past few days and had been caught. What was needed was an organized method of getting the refugees from their places of hiding to various collection points, and later handing them over to fishermen willing to take them across the sound to Sweden. It was also necessary to get the fishermen to set a uniform price. Lillelund suggested that the group speak to a fisherman he knew by the name of Nielsen. He was certain that Nielsen would put them in touch with key members of the Fishermen's Association who would be cooperative in getting the fishermen to adopt a low, uniform price.

When the meeting ended, the underground group had decided to use as collection points the various hospitals in Copenhagen where there were already thousands of Jews in hiding. Ambulances and taxis were selected as the best means of transportation to take the refugees to the boats. Mogens Staffeldt suggested that the back of his bookstore be used as one of the collection points. At first there was some opposition to this suggestion, but Danes are known for their sense of humor, and, upon reflection, the idea of using a store across the street from Gestapo Headquarters as a collection point for the Jewish refugees struck the younger Staffeldt, Lillelund, and even Truelsen, as an amusing challenge. They agreed to use the bookstore.

One of the first groups of refugees brought to the store consisted of twenty Danish Jews, about half of whom were young children.[2] Lillelund brought them there from the cellar of a friend's house, where they had been hiding. All of them were extremely frightened, and at about 1 A.M. one of the children broke into a fit of hysteria which became contagious. In a matter of minutes, half a dozen of the children were screaming at the tops of their lungs, and the parents could do nothing to calm them.

"He's very nervous," said the mother of the child who had started the ruckus. "We usually give him a sedative when he gets like this, but we're all out of them now."

"They could all use sedatives," said one of the other mothers.

Lillelund knew that he had to get something to quiet the children or the entire group would be discovered. His own physician was in Sweden, and the only other physicians he knew were located far from the bookstore. He quickly consulted the telephone directory and picked out the name of an unknown physician who lived only a few blocks away. Because it was well after curfew, he had to sneak along in the shadows of the buildings to avoid being picked up by German soldiers.

The physician appeared at the door in his nightshirt.

"Can I come in?" asked Lillelund.

"Who are you? What do you want?"

"It's an emergency."

The doctor was suspicious and did not budge. Lillelund knew in what contempt practically all of Denmark's physicians held the Germans, and without hesitation he quickly explained the situation. "So if you could just give me a bottle of sedatives or sleeping pills for the children, I'd appreciate it ever so much."

"Nonsense," said the doctor. "A thing like that needs a physician. I'll have to take care of it myself. If you take me to the children, I'll get them to keep quiet. Now come in while I get dressed."

"We don't have much time," warned Lillelund.

"All right," said the doctor. "Let me at least put an overcoat over my pajamas."

Hurriedly throwing an overcoat over his shoulders and grabbing his medical bag, the physician followed Lillelund to the back of Staffeldt's bookstore. The parents were frantic. The children were still screaming.

Working as quickly as he could, the doctor injected all of the children with a sedative that made them unconscious. They looked dead. Their parents turned white with apprehension. Lillelund found himself trembling.

"I know," said the doctor. "They look dead. But don't worry, they're not. If you look closely, you can see they're breathing."

Lillelund and the parents examined the children. They were breathing.

"They'll remain unconscious like that for from six to eight hours," explained the doctor.

Lillelund couldn't take his eyes off the children. Continuing to stare at them, he addressed the doctor: "What's your fee?"

"None," said the physician. He packed up his medical bag, threw his overcoat over his pajamas and left.

No one spoke. The parents of the unconscious children were deathly silent. Like Lillelund, they could not take their eyes off the children.

"I'm sure the doctor knew what he was doing," said Lillelund. "It's much better this way. Now nobody will hear them. And, as the doctor said, they'll snap out of it in from six to eight hours. We won't be going to the fishing boats before then."

"What if they start screaming again when they wake up?" asked one of the refugees. "What if they start screaming on the way to the boats?"

"They'll have to be injected again," replied Lillelund. "Maybe it's a good idea to inject them again just before leaving for the boats. They can be carried down to the boats. It'll be a lot safer that way."

One of the fathers, holding his unconscious son in his arms, began to sob.

"What have they done to deserve this?" he asked. "What do the Germans want with them? They're only children. Children . . ."

Lillelund hurriedly walked out of the back room into the bookstore proper. He could barely see as there was practically no light coming in from the blacked-out street. Somehow he made his way past the bookstacks to Staffeldt's desk. He sat down, buried his head in his arms, and then Jens Lillelund, a tough saboteur, cried.

Out of Lillelund's grim experience with the refugees whose hysterical children had to be drugged into unconsciousness came a valuable and regularly employed procedure, the sedation of all of the refugee children during the transportation to the boats and on the sea crossing to Sweden. In addition to the injections, the physicians often gagged and taped the mouths of the children, so that should the trip take longer than anticipated and the effect of the injections wear off, the children would still be quiet.

Word spread that Mogens Staffeldt's bookstore was a collecting point for the Jewish refugees, and, in addition to those Danish Jews who were brought into the store by members of Staffeldt's underground unit, many started coming in on their own. This resulted in a larger influx of refugees than had been anticipated, and, for assistance, Staffeldt enlisted the aid of his five employees. A signal had been decided upon to announce that the store was free of Germans. If a copy of Kaj Munk's poems was in the window, it meant the coast was clear. The absence of the book from the window meant that it was dangerous for Jews to enter the store. Arrangements were made with a number of dependable fishermen in Copenhagen Harbor. The Fishermen's Association got them to agree on a uniform price—about sixty dollars per passenger. During the day, the refugees were brought, or came themselves, into the store, and at night they were taken by ambulance from the store to small wooden shacks and warehouses near the docks south of Copenhagen. They usually left for Sweden the same night that they were taken to the docks, but, occasionally, when German patrols in the area were unusually heavy, the refugees had to remain hidden in the wooden shacks and warehouses for as long as two or three days. Whenever this occurred, it meant that Staffeldt's group had the additional problem of feeding the refugees.

For the Staffeldt group, not all of the incidents in getting the Jews to the boats were as disturbing as Lillelund's initial experience with the children who had to be drugged.

One night Staffeldt's group was asked to cooperate with another underground unit which had forty refugees it wanted to get to Sweden.[3] Lillelund and Staffeldt's younger brother Jørgen were taken by an agent from the other underground unit to an empty summer house on a beach south of Copenhagen. The agent informed them that after he left they were to remain hidden in the house for exactly half an hour, and were then to report to the rendezvous on the beach to which he would bring the refugees. The agent further explained that because of the German patrols on the beach, exact timing was of the utmost importance. Lillelund and Jørgen had to be at the appointed rendezvous *in exactly half an hour*.

After the agent departed, Lillelund looked at his watch and noticed that it had stopped running. He wound it and shook it to no avail.

"What time have you got?" he asked Jørgen. "My watch is broken."

Jørgen felt his wrist.

"I forgot to take my watch," he said.

"Oh, Jesus," said Lillelund. "How the hell will we know when the half-hour is up? Let's look around, maybe there's a clock somewhere in this summer house."

They desperately scampered around the house until Lillelund heard Jørgen cry out from the kitchen: "Our worries are over."

Lillelund ran into the kitchen, where he saw Jørgen gulping down a bottle of beer.

"Did you find a clock?" asked Lillelund.

"No," replied Jørgen. He held the bottle in the air. "But I found this."

"A fine time to drink beer," exploded Lillelund. "We need a watch and you—"

"This is just as good," interrupted Jørgen. He gulped down the remainder of the beer and smiled. "Have you ever seen me drink beer before?" he asked.

Now that Lillelund thought about it, he had never seen him drink beer.

"Do you know why?" asked Jørgen. "Because I seem to have some sort of allergy to it. Drinking beer is embarrassing to me because it gives me an uncontrollable urge to pee. My brother and I once timed it and we found this uncontrollable, irresistible urge came on exactly half an hour after I'd have a bottle. Believe me, it works like clockwork."

Lillelund and Jørgen went into the living room, where they sat in the dark and waited.

"Now?" asked Lillelund.

"Not yet," said Jørgen. "I can pee if I want to, but it's not that uncontrollable, irresistible urge."

After a few minutes, Jørgen jumped to his feet. "Now!" he said. "Let's go!"

They raced to the rendezvous on the beach. The forty refugees were also arriving at that precise moment, and Lillelund and Jørgen, with time out for Jørgen's call of nature, got them to the boats on schedule.

Several days after the incident on the beach, Staffeldt's group was involved in another episode with humorous overtones.[4] Arrangements had been made with a large fishing boat to take fourteen Jewish refugees to Sweden. Lillelund transferred them from the bookstore to a house in Nyhavn, the tough sailors' section on the Copenhagen docks. When he went to see the ship's captain to verify last-minute details, the captain unexpectedly expressed a fear: "I've got two new crew members," he said, "and I don't know if I can trust them."

"But you've about ten other crew members on board," pointed out Lillelund. "If the two start anything, the rest of you should be able to handle them."

"It's not that," said the captain. "I'm not worried about handling them during the trip. But what happens if after the trip they squeal to the Germans about what I've done? It'll mean my neck."

"But how can you back out at the last minute?" asked Lillelund. "You'll be jeopardizing the lives of fourteen people."

"I didn't say I wanted to back out," said the captain. "I've another scheme. The normal run of this boat is down to Germany. Instead of starting out for Sweden, what if I tell the crew that we're going to Germany, as usual. But then, once we get halfway there, suppose some of the refugees break out of the hold as though they were stowed away? I can arrange for them to get into the hold before any of the crew come on board."

"Then what?" asked Lillelund.

"Well, then they'll hold us up with guns, forcing us to take them to Sweden. In other words, it'll look like they're hijacking the ship."

"Do you really think all of that play acting is necessary?" asked Lillelund.

"Absolutely," replied the captain. "Then, in case the two new men turn out to be informers and inform on me, I can always say that I was forced to go to Sweden at gunpoint."

"But those Jews are a mild-mannered, gentle lot," pointed out Lillelund. "They don't know anything about weapons. Hell, they wouldn't even know at which end to hold a revolver."

"You could teach them," said the captain. "We've an hour before we sail. Teach them how to hold a gun and how to say 'Hand's up!' You'll have to do it fast because I want them on board and hidden before the crew arrives."

"What if the crew tries to disarm them?" asked Lillelund.

"Don't worry," said the captain. "I'll brief the whole crew on what's happening so they'll cooperate. I mean I'll tell the whole crew except for the two new men. Okay?"

Lillelund hesitated for a moment, then said, "Okay. If that's the only way you'll sail, okay."

He started to walk away when the captain called out, "Oh, one more thing." He ambled up to Lillelund and whispered; "Make sure there are no cartridges in the guns. I don't want those refugees getting nervous and shooting me."

Lillelund raced back to the store, got two pistols from Staffeldt, emptied them, and forced two unwilling refugees to learn how to hold them and shout "Hands up!"

The boat set sail on schedule, and several hours out of port, as planned, the two refugees came out of their places of hiding in the hold. The captain and the crew—except for the two new crew members—were expecting them, and, before the two refugees had a chance to draw their pistols or to say anything, the captain and his men had their hands high in the air and the captain was saying, "Don't shoot! We'll take you to Sweden, we'll do anything you want! Only don't shoot!" This was followed by the two nervous refugees drawing their pistols and stammering, "H-h-hands up!"

Several hours later, all fourteen Danish Jews were safe in Sweden. It turned out that the two new crew members were sympathetic to the plight of the refugees and eager to do everything they could to help them. All subsequent illegal trips this particular boat made to Sweden were without theatrics.

The members of Staffeldt's group admit that their work would not have been as effective as it was had it not been for the cooperation received from almost everyone with whom they came into contact. For example, at one time Lillelund was assigned to pick up four Danish Jews at the railroad station and bring them to the bookstore. In this particular operation an ambulance would have been too conspicuous, and so he decided to use a taxicab. Taxis were extremely scarce at that time, and when he and the refugees reached the street in front of the station they noticed that there were several people ahead of them who were also waiting for cabs. Finally, a taxi showed up and the man first in line approached it. The taxi driver, sensing somehow from their nervousness that the four people with Lillelund were Jews, turned to the man who was rightfully his passenger and said, "You were here first, so you can have the cab if you want it, but I think that the gentleman at the end of the line has a more urgent need for a taxi than you." The man took one look at the frightened refugees with Lillelund, sized up the situation, opened the door of the taxi and motioned for Lillelund and his charges to hurry in. There was not a single complaint from any of the other people on the line; instead, they nodded their approval.

Staffeldt's group had little or no contact with the other underground groups. This was deliberate, so that if one group was caught, its members could not be tortured by the Germans into revealing the membership and whereabouts of any of the other groups.

All in all the members of Staffeldt's group had nothing but complete respect for the way the Danish Jews behaved during their period of escape. According to Lillelund, they were all frightened, but, at the same time, they were courageous and often noble. The only times they became difficult, according to Lillelund, were on those occasions when there was not enough room for all of the members of a particular group in a single boat. Then the trouble would arise not because of a dearth of volunteers to stay behind, but, because nearly all of the adult members of the group would insist on remaining in Denmark while their fellow refugees went on ahead to Sweden. On one such occasion, an elderly man told Lillelund: "I'm seventy. Why should I go now? Maybe I'll die next year. This man is forty. Let him go in my place."

No accurate records were kept of the number of Jews who passed through Mogens Staffeldt's bookstore on their way to Sweden, but it is estimated that there were at least six hundred of them.

There were so many refugees passing through Mogens Staffeldt's shop during the October exodus that it resembled a travel agency more than it did a bookstore. In fact, during those days Staffeldt and his brother became quite annoyed and suspicious whenever someone entered who actually wanted to buy a book. It was the first and only time for Staffeldt since he had become a bookseller that no customers were wanted.

When asked why he helped the Jews to escape, Staffeldt replied: "I never think of a man as a Jew or not. It makes no difference to me. At that time I was helping people in trouble. I did the same for the Jews as I did for Allied fliers, saboteurs and others who had to get to Sweden."

Chapter 9 FIRST AID

> *You do solemnly swear . . . that you will lead your*
> *lives and practice your art in uprightness and honor*
> *. . . you holding yourselves far aloof from wrong,*
> *from corruption, from the tempting of others to vice;*
> *that whatsoever you shall see or hear of the lives of*
> *men which is not fitting to be spoken, you will keep*
> *inviolably secret.*
>
> THE OATH OF HIPPOCRATES
> CA. 400 B.C.

MOGENS STAFFELDT'S UNDERGROUND GROUP had
been accurate in its prediction that the hospitals would serve as
good collecting points and would be cooperative in supplying
ambulances and drivers for the transportation of the refugees.
No group did more to aid the Danish Jews than did the
Danish doctors. And no hospital did more than Bispebjerg
Hospital in Copenhagen.

Early in the morning on April 9, 1940, Dr. Karl Henry
Køster was awakened in his apartment on the grounds of
Bispebjerg Hospital by the sound of aircraft overhead. Noticing
that the planes in the sky were German, he thought at first that
Norway was going to be invaded. Then he observed that the

aircraft were not passing overhead but circling the city, and he knew that the country that was being invaded was his own. He felt neither surprise nor anger, only curiosity. Going into town, seeing the Germans with their Schmeisser machine pistols on street corners, he felt no fright, no resentment.[1]

Objective curiosity quickly gave way to personal loathing as Dr. Køster met Germans face to face. He knew that he would welcome any opportunity that presented itself for thwarting them.

His first opportunity came early in 1942, when he helped circulate the petition to the Danish government signed by sixty-four physicians on the staff of Bispebjerg Hospital promising cooperation if the government guaranteed no persecution of the Jews. His second opportunity came several weeks later when a Dane showed up in his apartment shortly before curfew. He was a big, hulking fellow, dressed in a workingman's cap and clothes. Dr. Køster was amazed at the calm expression on his face, because the front of his coat was soaked with blood pouring out of two holes in his stomach.

"You've got to help me," said the caller. "I'm a saboteur. I've been shot by the Germans while attempting to blow up a factory."

Dr. Køster hurried him inside, and while he examined him, the saboteur explained what happened. "I was the lookout. We were taken by surprise by a bunch of German soldiers. I wanted to give the boys inside time to get away, so I tried stalling them. I stood in the doorway and refused to let them pass. I told them that they'd have to shoot if they wanted to get me out of the way. That's just what they did. Twice in the gut. I fell down and played dead. After they rushed inside and were out of sight, I got to my feet, walked to the street and hopped a cab. Just as the cab was pulling away I saw the other boys make their getaway. My stalling worked. They didn't get one of us."

Dr. Køster called for an ambulance and had the saboteur

taken to the operating theater. He removed one bullet from his stomach and one from his liver, and admitted him into the hospital under a fictitious name, putting down on his medical chart that he was suffering from a perforated ulcer—which was technically correct.[2] When recovery was certain, and the saboteur was well enough to be moved, Dr. Køster, fearful that the Gestapo might trace him to Bispebjerg, had him transferred to another hospital.

Dr. Køster's third and most important opportunity to thwart the Germans came on October 7, 1943. On that day, Ole Secher, one of his medical students, paid him an unexpected visit.[3]

"Our student group has discovered forty Jews hiding out in the woods south of Copenhagen," said Secher. "We've made arrangements to have them taken by truck to some fishing boats tomorrow night, but there are quite a few Germans in the woods and we need a better place for the truck to make the pickup. Would it be possible for you to hide them here in the hospital for a couple of hours until the truck arrives to get them?"

"I'm sure we could," replied Dr. Køster. "But how would you get them here?"

"We've thought of that," replied Secher. "We'll stage a mock funeral, dress the Jews in black, have them carry flowers while following a hearse through Copenhagen to the cemetery on the hospital grounds."

"But the cemetery is small," commented Køster. "You can't have the truck pick them up there. It'll be too conspicuous. We often have Germans, including the Gestapo, on the hospital grounds. I suggest we keep them in the chapel until the truck comes for them."

"Perfect," said Secher. "We'll have the phony funeral procession go right from the front gate to the chapel. That's an excellent suggestion. You can expect the forty Jews here first thing tomorrow morning."

At 8:30 A.M. Køster received a telephone call from a distressed gatekeeper. "A whole bunch of Danes have just come in for a funeral," he said.

"Well," asked Køster, "what's so unusual about that?"

"We never have funerals here so early in the morning."

"Sometimes we do," said Køster.

"In the thirty-five years I've been gatekeeper we've never had a funeral here so early in the morning."

"But these are unusual times," said Dr. Køster. "We're under the German occupation."

"But nobody told me there was going to be a funeral here this morning," said the gatekeeper. "Why was I not informed?"

"I forgot to tell you," said Køster. "I had an emergency operation to perform last night and it must have slipped my mind. Yes, I meant to tell you to expect about forty mourners."

"There aren't forty," said the gatekeeper. "There are more than a hundred and forty!"

"Are you sure?"

"Yes."

"Well," said Dr. Køster, "let them through."

He ran down to the gate to see for himself, and there, sure enough, were at least 140 "mourners." Included among them was his student Ole Secher. Dr. Køster joined the funeral procession, marching next to Secher.

"What happened?"

"Some of them told others," said Secher, "and I couldn't very well tell any of them not to come. So here they are."

Slowly the funeral entourage made its way up the tree-lined path to the chapel on top of the hospital grounds.

"Have you made arrangements for transportation for the additional refugees?" asked Køster.

"No," said Secher. "There's only one truck for the forty refugees."

"Perhaps it can make two more trips."

"No," said Secher. "The arrangements we've made with the fishermen are for only forty refugees."

Over 140 refugees entered the chapel. A couple of hours

later a canvas-covered lorry entered the hospital grounds and drove up to the chapel. Forty refugees chosen at random were loaded inside the truck. As the last of the forty climbed on board, Dr. Køster noticed a Gestapo car pull up several hundred yards down the road.

"What'll we do?" he asked.

"What can we do?" replied Secher. "We'll have to hope they got there too late to notice anything." He signaled the driver to proceed.

As the truck pulled away, the canvas flap at the rear of the truck was suddenly pulled back and one of the refugee children, waving his hand, yelled, "Bye, bye everybody!" He then let the flap close.

The Gestapo car started following the truck.

Dr. Alan Gammeltoft, who had been working with Ole Secher in rescuing the refugees, said, "They might not have seen the refugees getting into the truck from the chapel, but they must have seen the little boy waving goodbye."

"Maybe they didn't," said Secher. "They were still down the road when it happened."

"Then why are they following the truck now?" asked Dr. Gammeltoft. "We had better not take any chances. I'm going to get into my automobile and ram the Gestapo car. I'll try to make it look like an accident."

He jumped into his automobile and gave pursuit. Outside the hospital grounds, just as Dr. Gammeltoft was about to slam his foot down on the accelerator and crash into the Gestapo car, it turned down another road.

Returning to the chapel with the good news, Dr. Gammeltoft found Dr. Køster and Ole Secher engrossed in trying to decide what to do with the one hundred refugees who had been left behind. They could not remain in the chapel. What was particularly distressing was that there was no way of knowing how long they would have to be kept on the hospital grounds. Obviously it would take at least a day or two for arrangements to be made to have them taken to Sweden. Meanwhile, there were the questions of housing and food. The doctors decided that the department of the hospital with the most room was the psychiatric building. It was also one of the least likely sections to be searched by the Germans. In groups of two and three, with spacings of at least five minutes between each group, the refugees were led from the chapel to the psychiatric building.

The following morning, Dr. Køster received another telephone call from the gatekeeper. "More mourners."

It came as a complete surprise to Dr. Køster. "How many?" "At least two hundred."

Dr. Køster wondered what the devil was wrong with Secher. Where could they possibly put two hundred additional refugees? There was no more room in the psychiatric building. After the new arrivals were in the chapel, Dr. Køster approached Head Nurse Signe Jansen.

"Do you think you might find room for some of these refugees in the nurses' quarters?"

"I'll speak to my nurses," said Nurse Jansen.[4]

A little while later Nurse Jansen returned to Dr. Køster with a huge batch of keys. "The nurses are willing," she said. "Here are the keys to thirty apartments in the nurses' quarters. Some of the nurses will stay in their apartments with the refugees, sleeping on the couch or on the floor. Others will double up with other nurses."

The two hundred new refugees were taken to the nurses' quarters. Later that afternoon Ole Secher showed up. He knew nothing about the new arrivals. "It must have spread by word of mouth that Bispebjerg is a good place to hide," he said.

"That means we can expect even more refugees."

"I suppose so," replied Secher.

That evening, before curfew, an additional hundred refugees showed up. Dr. Køster was no longer distressed. Bispebjerg *was* a good place for the refugees to hide. They could sleep in the nurses' quarters and be fed from the hospital kitchen. All that remained were the arrangements that had to be made with fishermen to take the refugees across to Sweden. This was done by Ole Secher. Contact was established with Mogens Staffeldt and other members of the resistance. The matter of transportation was solved by using Bispebjerg's ambulance fleet. One of the most effective ambulance drivers in this operation was Jørgen Knudsen. Together with several other drivers, Knudsen was taken off regular duty and during the period of the exodus he worked full time transporting the refugees. Another outstanding ambulance driver in the operation was Captain Kisling. In addition to transporting refugees hidden by his wife and himself in the attic above the garages of the salvage company for which he worked, Kisling served as a liaison man between Mogens Staffeldt's bookstore and Bispebjerg Hospital. Occasionally he transported the refugees in salvage trucks and fire engines instead of ambulances.

In a matter of days, Bispebjerg Hospital became one of the most important collection points for the refugees, with virtually the entire medical staff cooperating to save the lives of their fellow countrymen. The nurses put 130 apartments at the disposal of the refugees, and the only time Head Nurse Signe Jansen had complaints from her staff was when there were not enough refugees in the apartments. The nurses vied with each other in trying to help the Jews.

Dr. Køster described the nurses' cooperative attitude. "Many an elderly Miss who would usually get terribly upset if anyone put a finger on her polished mahogany table now found it completely natural that an entire family whom she didn't know occupied her flat. The father and mother, grandmother and an uncle slept on the sofa and in the chairs, while four small children peed in her bed. Her guests usually stayed for several days, and when they left, new ones came. She looked after them, fetched food and drink, got new clothes for them, and, most important, calmed them. She herself slept in the kitchen—when she slept at all."[5]

Not only did the doctors and nurses of Bispebjerg Hospital shelter the Danish Jews, but they participated in transporting them to the docks. Their work was not without danger. At times the Germans raided the docks, and several doctors and nurses were killed during such raids.

On one of his rescue missions, Jørgen Knudsen was picked up by the Germans and imprisoned for several days. He was beaten and tortured, but revealed no names. After his release from prison, he went back to saving the lives of more refugees.

On several occasions Dr. Køster accompanied the refugees to the docks. One night he was in charge of a group of more than 150 of them who were supposed to board a large fishing boat at Rødvig, about 42 miles south of Copenhagen. They were taken there in a fleet of about fifty taxicabs. On the beach they saw what they thought was the fishing boat and gave the signal agreed upon. A powerful searchlight from the boat hit the beach and suddenly a machine gun opened fire. By accident, the boat they had signaled was a German patrol vessel. Luckily, the fleet of taxicabs had not yet left to return to Copenhagen, and the refugees were able to race back into them. Dr. Køster ordered the taxis to drive to the southern tip of Zealand, and then over to the island of Møn, where he purchased a fishing boat to take the refugees to Sweden. All in all, it was an extremely expensive evening. The taxi fares came to over two thousand dollars, and the cost of the boat was twenty thousand dollars.[6] Fortunately, money was rarely a problem. When it became known how Bispebjerg Hospital was aiding in the rescue of the Danish Jews, money was freely donated to the hospital in both large and small amounts from people in all walks of life. This money, used for special contingencies such as the plight of the 150 refugees who had to leave from Møn instead of Rødvig, was kept in an open shoebox on top of Nurse Signe Jansen's desk. The amounts in it varied at different times from fifty cents to fifty thousand dollars. Among the heaviest contributors were the nurses themselves.

124   RESCUE IN DENMARK

Despite the risks, despite the raids and murders, the members
of the staff of Bispebjerg Hospital were relentless in their efforts to rescue the Danish Jews. During October over two
thousand Jews passed through Bispebjerg Hospital on their way
to freedom in Sweden.

Why did Dr. Køster work to save the Danish Jews? "It
was the natural thing to do. I would have helped any group of
Danes being persecuted. The Germans' picking on the Jews
made as much sense to me as picking on redheads."[7]
Why did Ole Secher? "We just had to. We—that means
some of my medical student friends and myself—just felt that
we had to do something about this particular situation. There
was nothing else we could do."
Why Nurse Jansen? "I was brought up to believe in democracy and to believe that you have to be willing to fight if you
want to preserve that democracy. As for helping the Jews,
I didn't feel any particular responsibility for Jews. As a matter
of fact, I never thought of them as Jews or anything else. They
were merely my countrymen and they needed my help."
And Jørgen Knudsen? "It was never a question of Jew or
non-Jew. It was a question of people in distress. I would have
helped anyone to escape from the Gestapo."

Toward the end of October, the Germans increased their
vigil at Bispebjerg Hospital, and the rescue of the Danish Jews
became more difficult. Occasionally, the Germans would raid
the operating theater of Bispebjerg Hospital, and when a doctor was found performing surgery on a Jewish patient, the
Germans would machine-gun to death patient, doctor and
everyone else in the room assisting the operation. One of Dr.
Køster's closest friends, an outstanding surgeon, was killed in
this fashion.

One night, toward the end of the rescue operation, two Germans in civilian clothes showed up at Køster's apartment.[8] His
wife answered the door.

"We would like to see your husband."

"He's not in."

"When will he be back?"

"I don't know." When Mrs. Køster tried to close the door, the two Germans pushed her aside. They signaled to four Germans waiting in the hallway, and the six of them entered the apartment. They calmly went about making themselves at home in the living room.

"What do you want here?" she asked. "This is not my husband's office. This is our private home. You have no right to come here without being invited."

"That's all right," said one of the Germans. "We intend to wait for your husband until he returns." He took from his pocket a small metal badge and showed it to her. It was the medallion of the Gestapo.

They waited for several hours, during which time two refugees entered the apartment to see Dr. Køster. The Germans, forced them at pistol point, to take seats in the living room.

"Who are these young men?" asked the Gestapo officer.

"They are medical students," lied Mrs. Køster. "They are taking a course in surgery from my husband."

"Very good," said the Gestapo officer. "That means that your husband should be home soon. We'll wait for him."

The doorbell rang, and when Mrs. Køster opened the door, in walked a young medical student she knew, Kato Bachmann. When the Germans ordered him to join them in the living room, he became very nervous. He had been working with Dr. Køster in the illegal transport of the refugees, and Mrs. Køster knew that three days before he had narrowly escaped a Gestapo trap.

One of the Germans noticed that Bachmann wore high leather boots. "Why are you wearing those boots?" he asked. "What have you got inside—illegal papers? Take them off. Let's have a look."

Bachmann stood up, but, instead of taking off his boots, he

made a dash for the window. He succeeded in opening it and leaping to the ground one floor below. The Germans, with guns drawn, got to the window as quickly as they could. Mrs. Køster tried to prevent them from shooting at Bachmann, but one of the Germans held her arms while another took careful aim and fired eight shots into Bachmann's back as he ran down the street, killing him.

At that very moment, Dr. Køster was on his way home. He was about 100 yards from the house when he heard the shots. He turned around and walked until he came to a restaurant, from which he telephoned his wife. He was surprised to hear her say, "Dr. Køster is not home. He won't be home until much later."

"I understand," said Dr. Køster, hanging up. He was not to speak to his wife again for almost three years—not until July 1946.

Back in the apartment, when it became obvious to the Germans that Dr. Køster would not show up, Mrs. Køster was placed under arrest and taken to Vestre Prison. Her first meal there consisted of money receipts and other papers and documents she had on her which she thought might be incriminating. After three weeks in Vestre Prison, during which time she was questioned daily but revealed no information, she was sent to the German prison at Hørserød, from which she was released two weeks later.

After receiving the warning from his wife over the telephone, Dr. Køster went straight to the home of his friend Peter Heering, owner of the well-known Cherry Heering factory outside of Copenhagen. He remained in hiding there for ten days, after which he was smuggled to Sweden aboard a schooner. In Stockholm, Køster contacted the British Embassy and offered his services to them as a doctor. The British Embassy arranged for him to get to London, like Niels Bohr, in the bomb bay of an R.A.F. "Mosquito."

While serving as a medical officer with the British armed

forces, Dr. Køster was among the first to enter the Bergen Belsen concentration camp in 1945. What he saw there convinced him more graphically than anything else possibly could that he had been right in helping to save the lives of two thousand Danish Jews.

It is impossible to relate all of the stories of heroic action by Danish doctors, nurses and other medical personnel in rescuing the Jews. Dr. Stephan Lund, an eye specialist at Kommunehospitalet, was particularly effective in raising money for the Jewish refugees.[9] Dr. Erik Husfeldt, professor at the University of Copenhagen Medical School, performed many courageous acts on their behalf. The medical students were equally helpful. Margrethe Florander, one of Dr. Husfeldt's students, led a protest strike of medical students against the German persecution of the Jews.

Bispebjerg Hospital was involved with the largest number of refugees, but there was hardly a hospital in Copenhagen that did not in some way or other actively participate in the rescue operation. Julius Margolinsky was hidden for several weeks, under the fictitious name of Julius Madsen, as a "mental patient" in the Philadelphia Hospital for Epileptical and Nervous Disorders in Copenhagen. Law Professor Stephan Hurwitz, now parliamentary commissioner of Denmark, was hidden in Frederiksberg Hospital, supposedly suffering from a mysterious stomach ailment. While there, he underwent so many painful stomach pumpings and examinations that he was tempted to give himself up. Fortunately, before yielding to his temptation, he was contacted by a member of the underground who arranged a far more comfortable hideout for him in Elsinore.

"Because the entire medical profession stood together as a single unit in opposition to anti-Semitism, our efforts in behalf of our countrymen of the Jewish faith were that much easier," said Dr. Køster. "We knew that the Germans couldn't arrest all of us."

Medical care is free in Denmark. For combating the disease of anti-Semitism which the Germans attempted to introduce into the country, the Danish doctors and nurses charged no fee. Their only payment was their satisfaction in knowing how importantly they had contributed to Denmark's testament to humanity—its rescue of its Jews.

Chapter 10 THE BOURGEOIS
HOUSEWIFE

The more the danger, the more the honor.

—JOHN FLETCHER

CLOSELY ALLIED TO DENMARK'S HOSPITALS in medical research is Copenhagen's celebrated Rockefeller Institute. In 1943 the Rockefeller Institute and the hospitals cooperated in still another endeavor—the rescue of the Danish Jews. One of the most effective members of the Rockefeller Institute group was Mrs. Ina Haxen, who was at the time according to her own description of herself, "a dutiful bourgeois housewife."[1]

Mrs. Haxen was born in Sweden of a Jewish father and Christian mother. In 1927 she emigrated to Denmark, where she married Ole Haxen, a Danish engineer. When the Germans invaded Denmark, Mrs. Haxen was thirty-three years old and the mother of three small children. She lived with her family in Aarhus, a town 150 miles northwest of Copenhagen. Her husband was wealthy, and the family occupied a huge house surrounded by a beautiful garden and tended by a staff of servants. Her only concerns were running the household and caring for her children. She had no interest in politics and never gave a thought to the fact that she was half-Jewish.

As the German occupation of Denmark progressed, Mrs. Haxen was forced to become more aware of her Jewish background. Occasionally some of the upper-class members of Aarhus society would journey to Germany for their vacations and come back with stories of the German persecution of the Jews. Much to Mrs. Haxen's astonishment, several of the voyagers returned with a not unsympathetic attitude toward what the Germans were doing. Occasionally Mrs. Haxen would hear something like, "Well, the Jews really have it coming to them. They behave badly."

"Do you know this for a fact?" Mrs. Haxen would ask. "Have you seen it for yourselves?"

"No," would be the reply. "It's what we've been told by the Germans. They claim the Jews always behave badly."

"Do you personally know any Jews?" Mrs. Haxen would ask.

"No, we never met any Jews."

"Well, now you have. I'm Jewish."

Mrs. Haxen was only half-Jewish, but so annoyed was she by these occasional evidences of anti-Jewish feeling that she felt compelled to pose as a full Jew. Invariably, often hearing her say that she was a Jew, those who had voiced sympathy for the German attitude denied that they were anti-Semitic, but Mrs. Haxen was convinced that they had caught the germ of racial hatred in their visits to Germany. What most offended Mrs. Haxen were those occasions when someone, thinking himself helpful, would remark, "You don't have to worry about the Germans. You don't look Jewish. And you're married to a Christian."

On October 4, 1943, Mrs. Haxen's husband told her the news he had received of the German roundup. He felt that it was essential for her to leave as soon as possible for Copenhagen. Because of his wife's Swedish background, Mr. Haxen was certain that his parents would be able to arrange for her to get a Swedish passport and to be allowed to remain in Sweden once she got there. Mrs. Haxen was reluctant to follow her husband's advice.

"I'm only half-Jewish," she said.

"It doesn't matter," he replied. "How do we know the Germans will allow even half-Jews to remain free? Besides, you've been telling everyone that you are a full Jew, and I am sure that they believe you. The Germans will probably raid Aarhus in a day or two. You'll be safer staying with my parents in Copenhagen."

Mrs. Haxen thought that her husband was behaving hysterically, but she left for Copenhagen.

On the train to Copenhagen she met her friend Mr. Posin, a Jewish tailor from Aarhus. He told her that he too was going to Copenhagen to hide, and gave her the address of an underground contact, Mr. Aage Hermann, a sixty-five-year-old Danish writer.

When Mrs. Haxen arrived in Copenhagen, instead of going immediately to her in-laws, with whom she had never felt comfortable, she telephoned a psychiatrist she knew. He told her to waste no time in getting to his office. She took a trolley car there and found the psychiatrist in an extremely agitated state.

"What's the matter with you!" he screamed at her. "How can you walk around the streets like that? Don't you know that all the Jews have gone into hiding and that the Germans are searching for them everywhere? My mental clinic is packed with Jews posing as patients. We've really no room for any additional refugees, but if you have no place else to go I suppose I could make room for you there."

"That's all right," said Mrs. Haxen, thinking of the address she had been given by the tailor Posin, "I've another contact."

"You better get over there as quickly as possible," advised
the psychiatrist.

As Mrs. Haxen started to leave, the psychiatrist stopped
her. "Just a minute," he said. "There is something I want
you to take with you." He unlocked a drawer of his desk, and
handed her a tiny pill box. "There's only one capsule inside,"
he explained. "It's cyanide. You might want to take it if captured by the Germans. From what we've learned recently, it
might be preferable to take your own life rather than face
what would await you in a German concentration camp."

She put the poison capsule in her pocket and walked out of
the office. Outside in the hall, she found herself trembling.
She sat on the steps of the staircase for a few moments to
collect her thoughts. How would she get to Aage Hermann's
apartment? What the psychiatrist had told her made her too
frightened to take a bus or taxi or even to walk. At the bottom of the staircase was a bicycle leaning against the hall
wall. She had never stolen anything in her entire life, but this
time she felt she had no other choice. Taking the bicycle,
she rode it to the address given her by Mr. Posin, the apartment of Aage Hermann.

When she arrived there, she had to identify herself as a
Jew and mention Posin's name to gain admittance. Posin was
inside, but completely changed.[2] She had never seen him
looking so downcast and glum. He led her into the living
room, which was crowded with about thirty Polish Jews who
had escaped to Denmark at the outbreak of the war.

"There's a Danish expression—'He looks like ten Jews.' "
explained Mrs. Haxen. "Well, each of these Polish refugees
looked like twenty Jews. I've never seen anything so sad
in all my life. These people had lost all hope. They just didn't
believe anyone could possibly want to help them. They sat
there as still as stones, just waiting for death. I felt like weep-
ing. They looked so afraid. For the first time in my life I felt
intensely Jewish. I wanted to kiss them all. I wanted to tell

them, 'Don't be afraid. I'll help you!' At that moment I decided come what may I would not go to Sweden. I would stay on in Denmark and do whatever I could to help my fellow Jews."

She told Mr. Hermann that she had no intention of escaping to Sweden, but wanted to stay on in Denmark to do what she could to help the others to escape. She wanted to know how she could be of service.

Hermann told her that his most pressing need at the moment was for money. He had made arrangements with a Danish fisherman to transport the Polish refugees to Sweden, but the fisherman wanted five thousand dollars to take them across, and this particular group of refugees was penniless. Mrs. Haxen, with her poison capsule and stolen bicycle, set out to see what she could do to ameliorate the financial crisis. Her first stop was her in-laws. Knowing them to be stingy, she decided against asking them for money for the refugees for fear they would turn her down. Instead, she told them that she had made her own arrangements to get across to Sweden, but needed five hundred dollars to pay the fisherman who was going to take her. They gave her the money, and she immediately turned it over to Hermann. She spent the next few days riding throughout Copenhagen on her bicycle, collecting money from relatives and friends. She did not repeat the ruse she had used with her in-laws of claiming it was for her own fare. She told them outright why she needed the money and their response was almost without exception quick and generous. In less than a week the Polish refugees had their fare for Sweden. In fact, Mrs. Haxen had collected five hundred dollars more than was needed.

"You can use it for the next group of refugees," said Mrs. Haxen to Hermann.

"There won't be any next group," said the sixty-five-year-old author. "At least not for me. I've become too nervous for this sort of thing."

"But what will I do with the extra five hundred dollars?" asked Mrs. Haxen. "And what about me? I want to continue doing whatever I can to help."

"Are you sure?" asked Hermann.

"Yes."

"You know what will happen to you if you get caught? You in particular will be able to expect no mercy because you are a Jew."

"I'm willing to take my chances."

"All right," said Hermann. "Go to the Rockefeller Institute. Ask for the head of the Biochemistry Department. His name is Professor Richard Ege. He can use both you and the money."

She left directly for the Institute.

Mrs. Haxen had no trouble getting to see Professor Ege in his private office. After she explained her mission to him and showed him the five hundred dollars, he brusquely asked her to leave.

"But why?"

"Because, young lady, you have made a mistake. You have come to the wrong person."

"But Mr. Hermann told me to see you. It was he who sent me here. He assured me that you were involved in smuggling Jews out of Denmark."

"I don't have the faintest notion of what you are talking about," said Professor Ege. "You have made a mistake, and I must ask you to leave."

Mrs. Haxen felt frustrated. It was obvious that Professor Ege did not trust her.

"I want to help," she said, "and you won't let me. I'm Jewish myself, but I don't want to go to Sweden. I want to remain here in Denmark and work with the underground. What can I do to make you believe me?"

Professor Ege's reply was to cross the room and open the door for her to leave.

Mrs. Haxen placed the five hundred dollars on Professor Ege's desk. "This money doesn't belong to me," she said. "It's supposed to be used for the refugees. You do whatever you like with it. Use it for your biochemical research if you like."

As she started for the door, she noticed a painting on the wall done by her uncle, the prominent Danish-Jewish painter, Ernst Goldschmidt.

"Oh, by the way," she said, "do you have any idea of what has happened to my uncle? I tried to get in touch with him, but he and his entire family have apparently disappeared."

"Your uncle?"

"Yes, Ernst Goldschmidt, the man who painted that picture."

Ege closed the door. "Sit down," he said. "Let's talk."

They talked for over an hour. Ege questioned her closely on details of Goldschmidt's life. He questioned her on her other relatives. It turned out that he knew one of her uncles, a chemist.

"Do you know this uncle well enough to visit him tonight?" asked Ege.

"Certainly."

"Good," said Ege. "Perhaps you ought to drop in on him tonight."

Mrs. Haxen left Professor Ege's office feeling optimistic. For one thing, the Professor had made no attempt to return the five hundred dollars she had left on his desk.

She entered a restaurant, telephoned her uncle and arranged to have dinner with him at his house that evening. At 8 P.M., just as her aunt started to serve the coffee, there was a knock on the door. In walked Ege. He had come to check on the veracity of Mrs. Haxen's story. They all had coffee together, and, from that moment on, Mrs. Haxen became a full-time member of Professor Ege's underground unit.

She learned that Professor Ege and his wife, the parents of

seven children, had overnight become the organizers and leaders of one of the most important of the underground units arranging for the transportation of Jews to Sweden. Like so many of their fellow Danes, the Eges had avoided participation in any Danish resistance activities until the German persecution of the Danish Jews had begun. Once alerted to the German raids by Professor Ege's associate, Dr. Poul Astrup, the Eges had put their huge apartment on the grounds of the Rockefeller Institute at the disposal of the refugees. As it became known that this apartment was a haven for those fleeing from the Germans, refugees quickly started showing up there in large numbers. Within a matter of days the Eges had over one hundred "house guests." The Professor persuaded his colleagues at the hospital attached to the Rockefeller Institute to allow some of the refugees to remain hidden there disguised as doctors, nurses and patients. As the numbers of refugees continued to increase, other hospitals were enlisted to help. At the beginning Professor Ege had no idea what he would do with all of the refugees, but, fortunately, Dr. Astrup put him in contact with several fishermen who were willing to take them to Sweden. Professor Ege soon found that his new transportation business allowed him little or no time for his research.

Most of the Jewish refugees with ample funds had managed to get to Sweden in the early days of the exodus. Professor Ege and his wife concentrated on those refugees who, because they were in a less fortunate financial position, were still in Denmark—the Jewish tailor, barber, shoemaker, government clerk. As seems to be the case throughout the world, it is always the poorest families that have the most children, and the Danish Jews were no exception. Families with six or seven offspring needed a substantial sum to pay the fishermen, even when the fares had been reduced to the uniform price of sixty dollars a passenger. Collecting money for these people was a large part of the work of the Eges. Fortunately, the wealthier

Danish Jews were willing to contribute large sums to help their poorer brethren. In addition, many wealthy non-Jewish Danes contributed handsomely. Professor Ege and his wife contributed their own savings, as did many of their co-workers. Careful records were kept of the money received and spent. Other records were kept with the names and locales of refugees still in hiding as well as those who had been safely transported to Sweden. Because of the danger involved should the records fall into the hands of the Germans, they were kept in a secret code—biochemical formulae decipherable only by Professor Ege. The money involved was kept in the laboratory, hidden at the bottom of buckets containing smelly, unappetizing chunks of food used by Professor Ege to feed his rats and guinea pigs.[3]

Despite the attempt to keep accounts, money was received and handed out with such casualness during the October exodus that it was impossible to think of it or deal with it in a normal manner. Occasionally contributions would be received by the Eges anonymously, and, on two occasions, Mrs. Ege was handed large sums of money by total strangers on the street.[4] On the second of these occasions, which followed the first by several hours, Mrs. Ege was walking along Juliane Mary Road when she was approached by a man unknown to her who asked, "Are you Mrs. Ege?"

When she replied in the affirmative, the stranger pulled two thousand dollars out of his pocket, handed it to her, and walked out of sight. Mrs. Ege went behind a bicycle shed, where she counted the money and hid it in the top of her stocking. Continuing along Juliane Mary Road toward her destination, she was stopped a few minutes later by another stranger. "You're Professor Ege's wife, aren't you?"

"Yes," she replied, half hoping for still a third anonymous contribution. But this time the stranger had no money to give her. On the contrary, he explained that he himself was involved in helping Jews out of the country and needed two thousand dollars desperately. Could she help? Mrs. Ege, feeling the man was telling the truth, asked him to turn his back to her for a moment. She reached under her skirt and took the money out of her stocking.

"All right, you can turn around now."

The young man was quite startled when Mrs. Ege put two thousand dollars into his hands and calmly continued on her way.

In addition to his wife and Mrs. Ina Haxen, Professor Ege had many effective assistants working with him on behalf of the Danish Jews. Dr. Poul Astrup was extremely helpful, as were Professors Brandt Rehberg and Linderstrøm-Lang, of the Rockefeller Institute. Other key members of his group included two Danish Jews, Mrs. Annemarie Glanner, Mrs. Ege's friend from Siam, and David Sompolinsky, a young veterinary student and an orthodox Jew. Despite the fact that, like Mrs. Haxen, they were in double jeopardy because they were Jewish, both worked as underground agents with Professor Ege until increased danger made it absolutely necessary for them to go to Sweden.

Most of Sompolinsky's activities were with an underground unit he had founded himself in Lyngby, a suburb of Copenhagen, but he also did a great deal of valuable work with Professor Ege's group. He had somehow gotten hold of one of the special blue uniforms of the civil police force, and, posing as a constable, went freely throughout Copenhagen after curfew searching out Jews, taking them to places of hiding, getting them to the fishing boats. During the month of October he slept no more than two hours a night, and, during all of his underground activities, to the occasional dismay and hardship of his underground associates, refused to eat any food that was not kosher. He often went without food for long stretches of time rather than violate the dietary laws of his religion. Finally, Mrs. Aage Bertelsen, wife of the leader of the Lyngby Group, concocted a special kosher food concentrate, consisting mainly of egg yokes and claret, which became his staple source of nourishment during his underground activities. Another of his religious observances involved shaving, and this was the cause of a serious dispute between him and Professor Ege, which all but resulted in his dismissal from underground activities.[5] While working with Professor Ege's group, he started to grow a beard. In 1943 the bohemians of Denmark had not yet discovered beards, and in general the only ones who grew them were orthodox Jews. Certainly no members of the civil police force were allowed to sport beards, and Sompolinsky was still employing the constable's uniform as a disguise. Professor Ege felt that the beard was a menace to the safety of the entire group.

"Do you realize what you look like, young man? Your face is a danger both to yourself and those around you."

When Sompolinsky refused to shave, Ege became furious and reported him to Aage Bertelsen, his superior in the Lyngby Group. He demanded that Bertelsen send Sompolinsky to Sweden immediately. Bertelsen refused on the grounds that his group could not operate without him. He approached the young orthodox Jew and insisted that he acquiesce to Professor Ege's demand to shave off his beard.

"Now look, David, get that beard off!"[6]

"All right. The only thing is that I shall have to go and get my razor first."

"Where?"

"In my apartment in Copenhagen."

"Under no circumstances! You will not leave this house until you have shaved! Now go into the bathroom and get that beard off. My razor is in there and everything else you may need."

"Thank you so much," said Sompolinsky, "but unfortunately it is impossible."

"What do you mean?"

"I cannot use your razor."

"Why not? It is probably just as good as your own!"

"No, it isn't."

"What the dickens is the matter? What is wrong with my razor?"

"I am not allowed to use that sort of thing," said Sompolinsky. "Moses has directed that we must not shave the beard—only cut it. You can look it up yourself."

Bertelsen was fast losing his patience. "Nonsense!" he shouted. "You are usually quite nicely shaved."

Sompolinsky pointed out that he used an electric razor.

"For heaven's sake," said Bertelsen, "then you do shave after all."

"No. An electric razor does not shave, it merely cuts the stubble."

After considerable difficulty, an electric razor was finally found—probably the only other one in Lyngby, and Sompolinsky was able to cut his stubble. More important, he was able to continue his disguise as a police constable and to continue to perform his important work for the underground.

Mrs. Ina Haxen's underground activities, in addition to collecting money for the refugees, consisted of acting as a courier. She contacted Jews in hiding and accompanied them to the Rockefeller Institute, and, later, to the back room of a restaurant, where another of Professor Ege's agents took them to the boats at the Copenhagen docks. She was never given the names of the refugees she was to pick up, in case of arrest by the Gestapo en route. On one such courier mission, the secrecy resulted in a rather unusual occurrence. Her assignment was to go to a villa in the west section of Copenhagen, where two young Jewish sisters were in hiding, and to bring them to Professor Ege's apartment at the Rockefeller Institute. When she reached the villa, she was surprised to see that the sisters were old school chums. They were as surprised and delighted to see her as she was to see them.

"How wonderful that you're in Copenhagen," remarked one of the sisters. "Come in and have some tea."

For the next half-hour the three of them sat around drinking tea, chatting and gossiping. As the minutes passed, Mrs. Haxen noticed that the girls grew more and more anxious.

"Is something the matter?"

One of the girls looked at her watch. "Yes," she replied. "Arrangements have been made for us to escape to Sweden. An underground agent was supposed to contact us half an hour ago, exactly the time that you arrived. In fact, when you rang the doorbell, we thought it might be the agent. I hope nothing has gone wrong."

"Oh, my God!" exclaimed Mrs. Haxen. "Seeing both of you made me forget why I've come here. I'm the underground agent you've been waiting for." And with that she hurried them out of the house to the Institute.

Toward the end of the second week in October, the crush of refugees became so heavy for Professor Ege that he decided to ascertain whether the Germans intended to arrest Danish half-Jews as well as full Jews. If not, the half-Jews could remain in Denmark at least until the full Jews were gotten to Sweden. It would make the entire rescue operation that much easier. At a meeting of the underground leaders, Mrs. Haxen came up with a suggestion for getting the information. Many years ago her family had befriended a young Dane who was ill and penniless, and nursed him back to health. This man had become one of the leading Danish Nazis, the right-hand man of Werner Best. She had not seen him in ten years, but, because of what her family had done for him, she felt that he might be cooperative and give her the information wanted by Professor Ege. The professor approved of her contacting him.

She telephoned him the next day and he agreed to see her that evening in his apartment.

His greeting could not have been friendlier. He seemed truly glad to see her. She tried to act friendly toward him despite her strong distaste for his Nazi uniform.

"I've come to ask you for a favor," she said. "I trust you so much that I'm going to ask you to help me. I'm half-Jewish, and I want to know if the Nazis intend to arrest, along with the full Jews, people like me, half-Jews."

He suddenly seemed less friendly. "I never knew you were a half-Jew," he said.

"Are we half-Jews to be arrested, too?"

"I don't know," he replied. "I'll have to ask Dr. Best about it tomorrow. How will I be able to get the answer to you? Where are you living?"

"You know I can't tell you that," she answered.

His face showed his annoyance at her response. "Why not?"

"I can't take a chance on getting the people I live with in trouble," replied Mrs. Haxen.

He flushed in anger. "Don't you trust me?" he demanded.

"It's not a question of trust," said Mrs. Haxen, "but I just can't give you the names of the people who are hiding me."

"But suppose I get the answer tomorrow from Dr. Best. How do you propose that I get it to you?"

"Leave a note for me at the newsstand in the Central Railroad Station. Messages are often posted there."

"I don't like the idea," he said. "I think it would be better if we met here again."

"But I'm half-Jewish," pointed out Mrs. Haxen. "You'd be taking a chance meeting someone like me."

"I'm willing to take it," he said.

"No," insisted Mrs. Haxen. "If you really want to help me you'll leave a note for me at the newsstand."

The Danish Nazi was so upset by this reply that the veins bulged on the side of his forehead. Mrs. Haxen became frightened at his anger. Suddenly he exploded. "It's because

you don't trust me," he shouted. "I can't stand your not trust-
ing me! You know how I have always liked you and your
family. Do you think I could ever forget what you did for
me? And now you don't even trust me. Do you think that's
fair?"

The idea of asking a Nazi for a favor suddenly struck Mrs.
Haxen as so loathsome an act, that, despite his fury, she
coolly replied, "How can I trust the enemy?"

He turned pale. Mrs. Haxen didn't want to go on, but
could not stop herself. "It's disgusting to find you here in a
Nazi uniform. How did you ever get mixed up in this revolt-
ing business? Can't you get out of it?"

Mrs. Haxen had never seen anyone turn so white. He said
nothing for a few moments. When he finally spoke, his voice
was unnaturally high: "It's too late." Slowly he lowered his
eyes and stared at the floor.

"You're not even on the winning side," she said. "The
Allies are going to win, you know."

"It's too late," he repeated.

"Goodbye," said Mrs. Haxen. As she left the apartment,
she knew she hated her former friend, hated him even more
than she could hate a German, but, at the same time, she could
not help but feel sorry for him.

Two days later she went to the newsstand at the Central
Railroad Station. As she approached the newsstand, it occurred to her that her former friend might have informed the
Germans about her, and a Gestapo agent might be nearby.
She decided to take a chance. She walked up to the news-
dealer, mentioned her name and asked if there were any
messages left for her. He handed her a note. She thanked him
and walked quickly away, attempting not to appear self-
conscious, trying to determine whether she was being followed. When she felt reasonably certain that no one was
spying on her, she opened the note, read its contents and tore
it into tiny pieces. Then she hurried to the apartment of

Professor Ege to tell him that for the time being the Germans had no intention of arresting half-Jews.

This information made it possible for Professor Ege to concentrate his efforts on the transportation of full Jews. By the end of October, he and his wife had arranged for the safe passage to Sweden of over a thousand Jews.

Why did the Eges help the Jews?

"It was exactly the same as having your neighbor's house on fire," said Professor Ege. "Naturally you wanted to do something about it. I never felt any danger. You see, I've always been an optimist, and so I never believed anything really bad could happen to me. There was only one time when I suppose I did feel a bit close to danger. It was the day we were forced to leave our apartment in the Rockefeller Institute and go into hiding under a pseudonym. We were together with our children in the apartment when there was a terrific banging on the door that meant only one thing, the Gestapo. We immediately went through a door that led directly to my laboratory, where I knew we could hide safely. The Germans broke in, but they were too late. They left half an hour later, and we were able to make our way safely out of the Institute."

Mrs. Ege said, "We helped the Jews because it meant that for once in your life you were doing something worth-while. There has been a lot of talk about how grateful the Jews should be to their fellow Danes for having saved their lives, but I think that the Danes should be equally grateful to the Jews for giving them an opportunity to do something decent and meaningful. It was a terrible time, but I must confess that it was also a wonderful time, a happy time. Yes, I don't think that we were ever happier. Our activities gave us a special feeling of oneness. We were together. Nowhere were we refused."

Chapter 11 THE LYNGBY GROUP

> *We do not congratulate a schoolteacher for teaching*
> *that two and two make four . . . But again and again*
> *there comes a time in history when the man who dares*
> *to say that two and two make four is punished with*
> *death.*
>
> —ALBERT CAMUS

BECAUSE OF THE HEAVY CONCENTRATION of Gestapo and Wehrmacht troops in Copenhagen, many Jews chose not to attempt the escape to Sweden from the capital, but instead left for a number of towns on the eastern coast. In many cases they were encouraged to do so by the underground in Copenhagen. To aid these Jews, there sprang up in the outlying areas several important rescue groups. One of these was located in a suburb of Copenhagen called Lyngby.[1]

The head of the Lyngby Group was a schoolteacher, but its founder was the young orthodox Jew David Sompolinsky. At the outbreak of the German raids, David had asked the principal and teachers of his former school, Christianshavn High School, whether they could help him hide a group of Jewish refugees. As a result of this request, which the headmaster and teachers immediately honored, the Lyngby Group was founded. Among the teachers asked to participate was one destined to become its leader, Aage Bertelsen.

During the first week of October, Bertelsen's semidetached house at 33A Buddinge Lane in Lyngby became known in the underground circles as "the house with the blue curtains." There was an incessant coming and going of cars and bicycles to and from the house, and its telephone rang day and night. With daring born of naïveté and inexperience, Bertelsen wanted as many Jews as possible to know about his willingness to help. "It was our wish that it should become universally known that here was a travel agency open any time and to anybody who felt impelled to go on a vacation to Sweden. We were well aware of the risk but we hoped that by the time the Germans got on our heels and closed down the shop we should have finished a useful piece of work."

On the telephone, however, Bertelsen and his wife did attempt to exercise some caution. They never mentioned Jews, but, instead, when making arrangements for transports, they referred to books, Carlsberg and Tuborg beers and movie tickets. Giving up teaching for the month of October, Bertelsen sent his two young children to the home of friends, and, with the able assistance of his wife, devoted his energies fully to the rescue of the Jews. Contacts were made with fishermen at Humlebæk and Smidstrup, and from Bertelsen's house Jews went into hiding, fed and cared for until it was time to take them to the boats. Transportation to the boats was usually by taxi, and one of the key taxi drivers in the Lyngby Group was a man by the name of Kjeldsen. Bertelsen came across him by accident during the first week of October, when he had gone into Copenhagen to collect contributions for the rescue operation from friends and acquaintances. Getting into a cab, he told the driver the addresses at which he wanted to stop. Kjeldsen informed him that he could be at his disposal for no more than three-quarters of an hour. Bertelsen agreed to the time limitation and they were off.

After half an hour, Bertelsen gave him his final destination—
Lyngby.

Kjeldsen became furious. "Absolutely impossible," he said.
"You'll have to get another car. Didn't I tell you that I could
drive you for three-quarters of an hour, and not a minute
more? Half an hour has already gone, and you damn well
ought to realize that I can't get to Lyngby and back again in
a quarter of an hour."

Bertelsen was in a hurry and knew how difficult it would
be to get another cab. "Shut up and drive," he said. "This is a
question of many human lives."

"Alright then," said Kjeldsen, changing his tone. "Now I
know what it's all about, and from now on you can count on
me, night and day! Yes, you're right. I don't know much
about Jews, but this is against my religion and my morals—
hunting people as if they were rats."

In addition to his wife, Sompolinsky and Kjeldsen, Bertelsen had a large number of other people assisting him. These
included quite a few teachers, several physicians, a hotel-
owner, a shoemaker and a trapeze artist. One of the most
colorful of the men he worked with was a Mexican sea captain who owned a large schooner which normally transported
trap rock. During the Spanish Civil War, the Mexican had
chartered his schooner alternately—depending on who would
pay the higher charter fee—to Fascists or Loyalists. With the
same objective financial attitude, he surmised that the Jews
would probably be a more profitable cargo than trap rock and
offered his services to the Lyngby Group. Despite his ad-
mittedly mercenary attitude, he was not unreasonable in the
prices he charged, and on one large transport took across 230
Jewish refugees for less than one hundred dollars a passenger.

The Lyngby Group operated during almost the entire
month of October. Its activities came to a sudden end on the
evening of October 28, as the result of the actions of a Danish
informer and pro-Nazi, Paul Hennig, who after the war

received a sentence of life imprisonment from the Danish courts. Posing as a saboteur who wanted to get to Sweden, he made arrangements with the Lyngby Group for passage across the sound. The night of the departure, as he was about to board the ship, he used his flashlight to signal some Gestapo men who were hiding nearby. They opened fire. The boat managed to get away and transport its Jewish passengers safely to Sweden. By some miracle, the members of the Lyngby Group involved in the operation also managed to escape the bullets of the Gestapo. But they had all been identified by the informer and they knew that their usefulness in transporting Jews was over and they themselves would now have to go into hiding.

Bertelsen and his wife went underground in the town of Stevns, where they were joined by their children. They had time to reflect on the events of the past month and they both agreed that regardless of what danger the future held in store for them they were most grateful for what they had just been through.

One day, discussing their activities in the Lyngby Group while walking down a road that ran along the cliffs, Mrs. Bertelsen turned to her husband and said, "It's as if we never realized before what it means to live."

Mrs. Bertelsen's reaction was not unlike that of her husband's two assistants. After the successful embarkation of refugees from Smidstrup, Bertelsen and Dr. Strandbygaard, a woman physician, were on the beach discussing their joy in their work, when the physician remarked: "Isn't this strange? Don't you think so? A very strange feeling! It's almost like experiencing again the overwhelming love of one's youth."

On the other occasion, after the dispatch from Humlebæk of some fishing boats containing Jews, several members of the Lyngby Group were walking on the beach when Speedy Larking, the trapeze artist, turned to the group's chief and said: "Do you know what I think I am feeling, Mr. Bertelsen?"

"Perhaps," said Bertelsen, "but tell me anyway."

"I feel—hang it—I feel like throwing myself down upon the road and saying, 'thank you!' "

On November 6, Mrs. Bertelsen left Stevns and returned to her home in Lyngby. Three days later she was arrested by the Germans and held as a hostage for the capture of her husband.

To German demands of information leading to the whereabouts of her husband, Mrs. Bertelsen replied that she did not have the vaguest idea of where he was now in hiding—which was true. And despite threats of harm to her children, she refused to reveal any information about her associates.

When it became evident to the Germans that holding Mrs. Bertelsen as a hostage would not lead to the capture of her husband—indeed, shortly after her imprisonment he had been smuggled by the underground to Sweden—they decided to let her go. On November 18, after signing a declaration that she would abstain in the future from any anti-German activities, she was released from Vestre Prison. Just before they let her go, the Germans questioned her about the Jews.

"We know you have participated in helping Jews to Sweden, isn't that true?"

"Of course it is," she answered calmly. "All decent people did."

"And why did *you* help the Jews? Was it to make money?"

"Because of sympathy with poor, persecuted people, who came to us confidently placing their lives and fates in our hands," she answered.

Chapter 12 THE ELSINORE SEWING CLUB

None can love freedom heartily but good men.

—John Milton

The winding 25-mile road along the seacoast from Copenhagen to Elsinore is perhaps the loveliest drive in all of Denmark. One passes striking vistas of the sound, several of the country's finest homes and resort inns, and charming woods of smooth-barked, glossy-leaved beech trees. It is particularly lovely in October, when the foliage changes colors. However, to the hundreds of Danish Jews who made the trip in 1943, there was little if any aesthetic delight in the scenic ride. These tense travelers were possessed by a single thought: escape.

Elsinore itself is one of Denmark's more picturesque towns, renowned for its famous Kronborg Castle, scene of Shakespeare's Hamlet. During World War II Elsinore was renowned for still another reason. It was the locale of one of Denmark's most effective underground units.

Like so many of the country's other underground groups, the one at Elsinore originated as a direct consequence of the

attempted German roundup of the Jews. Its five leaders—a
reporter, a bookbinder, a detective, a bookkeeper and a physician—all led law-abiding lives during the first years of the
occupation.

The day of the German invasion, Børge Rønne, a cor-
respondent in Elsinore for the Copenhagen newspaper *Ber-
lingske Tidende*, was awakened early in the morning by a
telephone call from a colleague.

"What do you think of the German planes?"

Rønne was half-asleep. "What German planes?"

"Look out of your window," said the colleague. "We're
being occupied by Germany."

Rønne was suddenly wide-awake. He had not expected it.
At the same time, he could not bother to worry about it. He
had other things on his mind, such as trying to find a new job
that would make it easier for him to support his wife and
daughter. During the first three years of the occupation he
kept his nose out of trouble and, changing to a better-paying
job as a reporter for the *Frederiksborg Amts Avis*, concentrated on his career in nonpolitical journalism.[1]

Erling Kiær, a bookbinder, did not have to be awakened by
a telephone call the day the Germans invaded his country.
He was stirred out of sleep by the sound of the planes. When
he looked out of the window and saw that they were German
bombers, he was neither particularly surprised nor disturbed.
As a matter of fact, he had anticipated their arrival, thinking
all along that the cowardly attitude of the weak Danish
government was tantamount to an open invitation for the
Germans to take over the country. He went back to bed and
slept soundly until seven o'clock. Then he arose, dressed and
rode his bicycle to the center of Elsinore, where he was dis-
heartened to learn that the Danish government had capitulated
after a loss of only thirteen lives. He was of the opinion that
it would have been more honorable if the Danes had lost
100,000 lives. Nevertheless, considering himself a man who

adapts easily to new situations, he had no difficulty adapting for the next three years to peaceful coexistence with the German invaders.[2]

In like manner, Thomod Larsen, a detective, Ove Bruhn, a bookkeeper, and Jørgen Gersfelt, a physician, went about their normal everyday lives during the first three years of the occupation.[3]

When the Germans decided to apply the Final Solution to Denmark, Børge Rønne was passing a friend's house in Elsinore, and noticed ten strangers leaping out of two taxicabs and running into the garage attached to the house. Rønne immediately rang the doorbell and told his friend what he had seen.

"It's all right," was the explanation. "They're Jews who have come to Elsinore to escape the Nazi roundup."

This was the first that Rønne had heard of the Jewish persecution in Denmark. Without having to think twice about it, he knew he would do everything he could to help get these refugees to Sweden.

A few hours later he bumped into Erling Kiær, an acquaintance. Kiær was deeply upset by something that had taken place the night before in his neighborhood—the shooting at random by German soldiers into open windows of Danish homes. It was, Kiær explained, a German reprisal for the Danes in the neighborhood having shaved the heads of girls caught fraternizing with German soldiers.

"We've got to do something to fix those Germans," said Kiær.

Rønne passed on to Kiær the news he had learned about the raids to arrest the Jews. "How about helping the Jews to get across to Sweden?" asked Rønne. "That would be one way of getting back at the Germans."

Kiær was immediately enthusiastic over the idea. "Yes," he agreed, "that *would* be a hell of a way to get back at them!"

"We would also be doing a very humane thing in helping our fellow countrymen of the Jewish faith," said Rønne.

"Don't give me any of that!" snapped back Kiær. "I don't give a damn about the Jews one way or the other. I'm only interested in seeing what I can do to annoy the Germans. I think it'll be great sport to see how many times we can fool them."

That meeting was the beginning of the Elsinore group. Rønne and Kiær, knowing that they needed additional members, contacted Thomod Larsen. They felt that Larsen would be particularly valuable to them because, as a police officer, he had access to confidential reports about refugees, underground groups and, even more important, the disposition in Elsinore and vicinity of Wehrmacht and Gestapo contingents. For additional assistance, Larsen enlisted the aid of Ove Bruhn. Fishermen were contacted who agreed to cooperate, providing some means could be found to keep Jewish children from crying or screaming while aboard the boats. To eliminate these qualms of the fishermen, Rønne and Kiær approached Dr. Jørgen Gersfelt, who practiced in the nearby fishing village of Snekkersten. Gersfelt agreed to help them, and the nucleus of the group was now complete. They called themselves, as a cover name, "The Elsinore Sewing Club."

At the beginning, the Elsinore Sewing Club concerned itself solely with locating safe places of hiding for the Jews and arranging their transportation to the fishing boats. H. C. Thomsen, owner of the Snekkersten Inn, a resort hotel at Snekkersten, was extremely helpful to the group in offering his inn as a hideout. He also secured places for the Jews at nearby private homes and empty summer houses.

When the time arrived for the Elsinore Sewing Club's first transport to Sweden, Dr. Gersfelt was extremely anxious. Charged with keeping the children quiet for several hours, he knew that sleeping pills would not be sufficient for the rough handling they were sure to have in their crossing. A

strong narcotic had to be administered, and Dr. Gersfelt, in-
experienced with the effect of such narcotics on children,
was fearful of the possibility of harmful aftereffects, especially
upon the infants. He was also uncertain of the proper dosage
to administer. He finally chose Luminal and picked what he
considered an effective, but safe, dosage. The children were
injected, the boat set out for Sweden, and Gersfelt remained
in agony until reports came back that the Luminal had
worked effectively and without any unfortunate aftereffects.
It was with considerably more self-assurance and ease of
conscience that Dr. Gersfelt injected subsequent groups of
children.

Dr. Gersfelt volunteered to aid the Club not only by giving
injections, but by acting as a driver for the refugees. The
fact that he was a physician meant that he had extra gasoline
rations for his small English automobile. As passengers he
concentrated on children and older people who had difficulty
walking. He rarely met German patrols on his trips, mainly
because he used back roads which the Germans had difficulty
locating. On the rare occasions when he was hailed by German soldiers, he drove past them pretending not to hear. He
also made sure to drive too rapidly for anyone to be able to
read the number on his license plate, which, as an added pre-
caution, he kept streaked with mud. In addition to his services
as a doctor and a driver, Gersfelt contributed to the Elsinore
Sewing Club keys to friends' summer homes at Snekkersten.
These keys were in his possession because it was his custom to
keep an eye on the summer homes during the winter. Feeling
certain that his friends would not object to turning over their
houses to the refugees, he did not even bother to contact them
for permission. After the exodus was over, he told his friends
what he had done, and not a single one objected.[4]

Elsinore seemed an ideal place from which the refugees
could cross to Sweden, since the sound separating Denmark
and Sweden at that point is only two and a half miles wide.

For this reason, Elsinore became an extremely popular point of departure for the refugees. However, as more and more of them began pouring into the town, it became increasingly difficult to arrange transportation for them. Because of the narrowness of the sound, it was relatively easy for German boats to patrol the area, and there were not enough daring fishermen to meet the heavy supply of passengers.

To help overcome the sudden rush of refugees, the Elsinore Sewing Club devised a scheme to get the Jews to Sweden by a means of transportation other than fishing vessels. An important ferry crossing for German railroad trains journeying between Denmark and Sweden was located in Elsinore. On the trip from Sweden, the trains were filled with iron ore and other important war materials, but on the way to Sweden they were generally empty. These empty trains were always locked, but there was enough of a wait at Elsinore before the trains were loaded onto the ferries for the Danes to open them and sneak Jewish refugees into them. Once in Sweden, the Jews would be given refuge by the Swedish authorities, who, it was hoped, because of their recently expressed sympathetic attitude toward the refugees, would keep their unique means of arrival a secret.

This method of transporting the Jews to Sweden succeeded for several weeks until a Swedish newspaper indiscreetly published a long, detailed article on the subject and the Gestapo put a special guard on all empty trains to Sweden. The operation had to be abandoned, and the Elsinore Sewing Club was forced to fall back upon the fishermen.[5]

The work of the Elsinore Sewing Club became increasingly difficult as the days went by. Delays had an unfortunate effect upon the morale of the refugees. One evening two groups of Danish Jews, one from Snekkersten and the other from Espergærde, were to meet in the woods at a point halfway between the two towns. As one group heard the other coming, each thought the others were the Germans, and, seized by panic, the members of both groups scattered throughout the woods. It took several days to gather them together again and calm them.

On another occasion, a far more tragic incident occurred as a result of delay. A group of refugees were hiding in the woods along the coast outside Elsinore. Hours passed without any sign of the boat for which they were waiting. The refugees became increasingly anxious. Rønne, who was attached to the group, suddenly had his conversation with another underground agent interrupted by the terrifying screams of a number of the refugees. Turning around, he saw that one of them, a brilliant young scientist, had run amuk. Holding an open razor in his hand, the scientist had cut his own throat and the blood was gushing from him. Several of the underground men managed to grab him, tear the razor away, inject him with a sedative and stop the bleeding. However, the screaming and wailing of the other refugees still continued. When Rønne went to investigate, he found the dreadful cause. Before attempting to kill himself, the young scientist had slit the throats of his wife and children and the three of them now lay dead in a pool of their own blood at the foot of a tree.

Later, when the scientist regained consciousness, Rønne learned what had happened. Despondent over the delay in getting a boat, fearing they would be captured by the Germans, knowing what lay in store for them if captured, the scientist and his wife had agreed upon a suicide pact. Walking away from the other refugees, they hid behind some trees. While his wife held their children in her arms, he killed them, then her. As he started to cut his own throat, his courage failed him.

Ironically, it was only a matter of hours after the tragedy that the boat assigned to take this group of refugees to Sweden finally arrived. The scientist was placed on board together with the others and, upon arrival in Sweden, was rushed to a hospital. There it was discovered that the physical damage he had inflicted upon himself was slight in comparison to the mental damage. He was transferred to an insane asylum, where he remained for several years. He is now back in Denmark, working as a scientist.

Because of fear that the Germans might discover the large concentration of refugees in their area, the Elsinore Sewing Club expanded their base of operations to include fishermen from the nearby towns of Espergærde and Gilleleje. This involved particularly hazardous problems of land transportation.

On one crossing, arrangements were made at Gilleleje for one hundred Jews to be taken over in a large schooner. From their hideouts in Snekkersten, they were taken after midnight in a convoy of four trucks and three private automobiles to a farm two miles from the Gilleleje harbor. Leaving the refugees at the farm, Kiær and Rønne set out by foot for the harbor to make sure that all last-minute details were set. The going was awkward for Kiær, because the ten thousand dollars he had with which to pay the fisherman was sewn into the lining of his coat in small bundles of coins and of bills of small denominations. Arriving at their destination, Kiær and Rønne knocked at the door of their underground contact. There was no answer. They were puzzled. Surely the contact knew that they were coming? They were persistent in their knocking. Finally, the contact came to the door. Even in the dark they could see that his face was chalk-white with fear.

"Why didn't you answer?" asked Kiær.

"I thought you were the Gestapo."

"You knew we were coming."

The man's eyes darted back and forth nervously. "Everything's off," he said, spitting the words out as quickly as he could. "The place is crawling with Gestapo! They've found out about the whole setup here! You've got to get away as fast as you can!"

As he slammed the door in their faces, they heard an automobile filled with Gestapo officers pull up outside. Kiær and
Rønne dove over the garden wall, jumped over several hedges
and made for the open fields. For Kiær, burdened as he was
with the money sewn in the lining of his coat, it was a particularly grueling getaway. They could hear the arrival of
more Gestapo cars and see the beams of flashlights trying to
find them. Knowing the area as well as they did, they were
able to avoid taking any roads to get back to the farm. They
crawled for several hours on their bellies through open fields
of mud and dirt until they arrived back at the farm. The
refugees were waiting for them in a state of extreme nervousness and tension. Would they get to Sweden that night?
What Kiær told them was of no comfort. There would be no
sailing. Instead, they had to return to Snekkersten immediately. The drivers of the trucks and automobiles objected. It
was too dangerous, they said. Kiær gave them some of the
money in the lining of his coat and the drivers changed their
minds. As the refugees started re-entering the trucks and
automobiles, a mother and her teen-age daughter suddenly
decided against returning to Snekkersten on the grounds that
the drivers had been right—it was too dangerous. This started
a panic among the other refugees. Kiær pointed out that if
the Gestapo were really as thick in the area as his contact in
Gilleleje had indicated, it was a matter of only minutes before
they might arrive at the farm. The refugees were still reluctant to leave. Kiær finally managed to persuade them to
change their minds by stating that he thought the trip back
would be so safe that he was willing to hazard riding in the
very first car of the caravan, thus risking certain capture if
stopped by the Germans. This bit of bravado seemed to calm
the fears of all of the refugees but the mother and daughter,
who elected to remain behind on the farm. With headlights
off and at top speed the seven vehicles raced back to Snekkersten. Later, Kiær learned from the farmer at Gilleleje that

several minutes after the departure of the vehicles the Gestapo
had arrived and arrested the mother and daughter who had
remained behind.[6]

What with the tragedies and the near-tragedies, the insufficient numbers of fishing boats and the heartbreaking delays,
the members of the Elsinore Sewing Club knew that their
operation could not go on with its present methods.

"We can't depend solely on the fishermen," said Kiær.
"We need our own boat to run full time."

"It would help," agreed Rønne, "but even if we managed
to get one, who would run it?"

Kiær pointed to himself.

"Do you know how?" asked Rønne.

"I've never run a boat in my life," said Kiær, "but I'm sure
I could learn. It would be fun."

"It would be dangerous. You've a wife and two small
children. And what about your business?"

"My wife and children know I like sports. Fooling the
Gestapo is the most exciting sport I can think of. As for the
business, the clerks can run it."

"This discussion is ridiculous," said Larsen. "There is not
the slightest possibility of our getting a boat."

"But if we *could* get one," asked Kiær, "would all of you
agree to let me be its captain?"

To humor him, they agreed.

The next day Kiær announced that he had procured a boat.
The club members were startled. They were even more
startled when he calmly stated that he had stolen it. There
were stern reprimands, but that evening Kiær made his first
trip to Sweden. To celebrate the success of the voyage—he
had taken ten refugees safely across—he checked into the
Grand Hotel in Hälsingborg and ordered a first-class Swedish
meal. The following morning he returned to Denmark and
made three more crossings with refugees to Sweden.

Several days later, a wealthy Jewish physician donated a

large sum of money to the Elsinore Sewing Club in appreciation for their having transported him and his daughter to
Sweden, and, on Kiær's insistence, the Club used the donation
as the down payment on a fast speedboat. The stolen boat
was returned to its owner, who was unaware that the boat
had ever been missing. With contributions from the local
townspeople, a second, larger boat was purchased. Averaging
a minimum of three or four crossings daily, "Captain" Kiær
quickly solved the transportation problem of the Elsinore
Sewing Club. A steady stream of Jews went from Elsinore in
Denmark to Hälsingborg in Sweden, and Kiær became an
elusive, seagoing Danish Pimpernel, vainly sought after by
the Gestapo.

To help stop the flow of refugees to Sweden a high-
ranking Gestapo officer and personal friend of Heinrich
Himmler was assigned to Elsinore.

One of the first places Gestapo Officer Juhl went to was
the Snekkersten Inn. Thomsen assured him that he had been
hiding no Jews and knew of no one else who had been hiding
them.

"If you're lying . . ." warned Juhl.

"But I assure you I'm not," Thomsen replied.

"All right," said Juhl. "You can prove to me that you're
not lying by being cooperative. The next time any guests
arrive whom you suspect may be Jewish, telephone me
immediately."

After Juhl departed, Thomsen contacted the Elsinore Sewing Club, and it was agreed to stop using the Snekkersten Inn
as a hideout.

Several nights later, a man showed up at the inn who
Thomsen was certain was Jewish.

"We're under surveillance by the Gestapo," Thomsen
warned the man. "For the time being we're not allowing any
Jews to stay here."

"Nonsense," replied the man.

"But it's for your own safety."

"But I'm not one of those lousy Jews," said the man, producing papers to show that he was an Aryan. "Sometimes I'm taken for one of them," he said, "but, as you can see, I'm not, thank God!"

Thomsen did not like the man's attitude and, for a moment, considered refusing him accommodations. On second thought, he was struck with a much better idea. In the small hours of the morning, he placed a call to Gestapo Headquarters at Elsinore, asking to speak to Juhl. The Gestapo chief, he was told, was at home sleeping. When he insisted that it was a matter of the utmost importance, he was given Juhl's private number.

"Sorry to wake you up, Herr Juhl," said Thomsen, "but I'm sure we have what you're looking for at the inn. The man who just checked in couldn't be anything but Jewish."

"Thank you for the information," said Juhl. "I'll be right over."

Juhl and several other Gestapo officers arrived at the inn a few minutes later. Thomsen accompanied them to the guest's room. He was fast asleep as they entered. Juhl tiptoed over to the bed.

"There's no doubt about it," said Juhl gleefully. "He's a Jew all right." He bent down and slapped him hard across the face. "Okay, Jew boy," he shouted. "Get up, Jew boy!" His subordinates laughed.

A few moments later, after examining the livid guest's identification papers, an embarrassed Gestapo chief took leave of Snekkersten Inn. Shaking hands goodbye with Thomsen, Juhl said, "Even though it didn't work out this time, don't think I fail to appreciate your telephoning me. Next time we'll get one of them, maybe more. Anytime you're suspicious, telephone me. Any hour of the day or night, it doesn't matter."

When Thomsen reported the incident to the members of

the Elsinore Sewing Club, they decided that it would be most amusing to plague Juhl by taking him at his word. Consequently, he was called to Snekkersten Inn and a number of other places at a variety of odd hours. So harassed was he by these calls that one night, after a heavy drinking bout, he announced to Thomsen: "I'm afraid that the pistol that finally ends my life is to be found right here in your damned Snekkersten Inn."[7]

Despite his failure to keep himself from being the butt of many a Danish practical joke, Juhl was not a complete idiot, and slowly but surely he began closing in on the Elsinore Sewing Club.

During one raid on an Elsinore hideout, reporter Rønne and a group of refugees in his charge missed being caught by Juhl by a matter of seconds. Luckily Rønne had in his pocket a pair of scissors which he normally used for newspaper clippings. With the Germans hot on his heels, Rønne used the scissors to cut through a wire fence surrounding a large chicken farm. The refugees were then able to hide themselves safely among the many chicken coops on the farm. Rønne, however, had been spotted, and the next day was arrested by the Germans. For several weeks he was confined to Vestre Prison in Copenhagen, where he was subjected to relentless questioning. He not only denied having participated in the escape to the chicken farm, but pretended to have no knowledge of the existence of Jews in Denmark. After several weeks, Rønne was released. On the day of his release, a Gestapo officer told him: "I really don't believe you know what's going on. You are one of the stupidest fools I have ever met."

After most of the Jewish refugees were safe in Sweden, the Elsinore Sewing Club decided to continue its transportation activities for the benefit of saboteurs, of Danes wanted for political crimes, and of English and American airmen who had been shot down over Denmark while flying to or from bombing missions over Germany.

On January 20, 1944, Larsen was on the beach at Snekkersten awaiting the arrival of a fishing boat. Hiding in a summer house near the beach were the passengers for the boat—several young Danish Jews who had remained behind to work in the underground, and two saboteurs. As Larsen peered into the darkness to see signs of the boat, he heard a voice behind him command in German: "Raise your hands!"

He did as he was told.

"You may turn around now."

He saw several German soldiers with their guns trained on him. Suddenly one of the Germans shot four times. Larsen fell to the ground critically wounded.

"You stupid fool," said Larsen, "you've shot a Danish police officer. I was out after curfew because I'm a police officer."

The Germans seemed puzzled. "We were told an important underground leader was here on the beach," said the German who had shot him.

"I'm a police officer," said Larsen, "a detective."

"You can be a police officer and, at the same time, an underground leader," said the German.

"That's still no reason to shoot me down in cold blood," said Larsen. "Why did you do that?"

The German did not reply. He held his pistol motionless. Larsen was surprised that he did not finish him off.

"What are you going to do," asked Larsen, "just stand there and let me bleed to death?"

For several minutes the Germans made no move.

"You filthy swine!" screamed Larsen. "All of you! Nothing but a pack of swine! Why don't you help me?"

One of the Germans made a move toward him, but the officer in charge motioned him back. In the distance could be heard the wail of a siren. One of Larsen's underground

associates had witnessed the shooting from a distance and had
sent a Danish ambulance to the beach. The ambulance took
Larsen to a hospital in Elsinore. Although he was placed
under a twenty-four-German guard, Larsen was smuggled by
members of the Sewing Club out of the Elsinore hospital and
driven in Christian Kisling's ambulance to Bispebjerg Hospital in Copenhagen. From Bispebjerg he was transferred to a
military hospital where he was registered under a false name.
The Germans, meanwhile, announced in the press that he had
been killed by them while attempting to escape. Actually, he
was not very far from death. The doctors gave him less than
a 10 percent chance of recovering from his severe wounds.
His close friend Ove Bruhn, despite warnings from the Sewing Club that it was dangerous to do so, visited him daily, and,
during the first weeks following the shooting, reported to
Kiær and Gersfelt that he thought it would be much better if
Larsen died and suffered no more. Despite the slim chances
given him for survival, Larsen, after many operations, re-
covered sufficiently to be smuggled to Sweden. There he
underwent still more operations. The Swedish physicians
were as pessimistic as their Danish colleagues on Larsen's possibilities for recovery, but he is still alive today, still working
as a detective, married and the father of a large family. He
feels that Ove Bruhn's friendship and loyalty gave him the
will to live.

The same night that Larsen was shot by the Germans,
Rønne's apartment was raided. His brother answered the
door, giving Rønne a chance to escape through the back door
and over the rooftops. The following day he went into hiding
in the home of another member of the Sewing Club, and,
several days later, was smuggled to Sweden.

The functioning of the Elsinore Sewing Club was now
seriously impaired. It was obvious that an informer had told
the Germans of the activities of Larsen and Rønne. Investiga-
tion revealed that not one, but *two* informers were involved

—O. I. Madsen, a police officer who worked with Larsen, and a naturalized Danish citizen known as "The Vienna Boy" because he had been born in Vienna and had come to Denmark after World War I as a war orphan. Madsen was given what the Elsinore Sewing Club called "a halfway ticket to Sweden." He was taken out in a boat, and, halfway between Denmark and Sweden, he was strangled and his weighted body thrown overboard. "The Vienna Boy" was tracked down in his apartment, where, in the middle of a luxurious dinner, obviously bought with the aid of German money, he was machine-gunned to death. The members of the Elsinore Sewing Club who carried out the execution felt not the slightest remorse over killing "The Vienna Boy," but their consciences did bother them because of the damage they had done to the apartment. They left a note for the landlord: "Sorry for the holes in the walls."

In spite of the near capture of Larsen and Rønne, the Elsinore Sewing Club's operations continued. Kiær's wife and two children were sent by the underground to Sweden, but Kiær continued his trips between Sweden and Denmark. On March 12, 1944, Kiær and a sixteen-year-old assistant were on their way from Hälsingborg to Elsinore in the speedboat. Entering the Danish waters, Kiær spotted a fleet of German patrol boats ahead of him. He spun the boat around toward Sweden only to see four German patrol boats gaining on him from this other direction. He ordered his assistant to lie flat on the bottom of the boat and raced the engine as fast as it would go, hoping to be able to pass through the four German boats and make it back to Sweden. The Germans opened fire immediately. With bullets whizzing around him, Kiær held one hand on the wheel to keep steady on his course, while, with the other hand, he threw overboard his pistol, a briefcase containing compromising papers, and American cigarettes and tobacco meant for Thomod Larsen, who was still wounded and in hiding in the military hospital in Copenhagen. Passing between two of the patrol boats, Kiær's engine suddenly stalled. A German bullet had hit the fuel feed line. As four German sailors boarded the speedboat, Kiær saw with dismay that his briefcase was still floating on the water. Unfortunately, one of the Germans also spotted it and it was fished out. At Gestapo headquarters in Elsinore, Kiær was tortured, but revealed no information of importance to the Germans. After spending several weeks in Vestre Prison in Copenhagen, where he again underwent torture without revealing anything, he was sent, together with several thousand other Danish members of the resistance, to Germany, first to the Neuengamme Concentration Camp, then to the Porta Concentration Camp. At Porta, he was made a slave laborer in the slate mines, contracting a serious lung condition from which he still suffers today. Because of lack of food, brutal treatment and the hard work in the ice-cold water of the slate-mines, death among Kiær's fellow prisoners was a common occurrence. "In Porta Concentration Camp at that time a Dane died every third day," explained Kiær. "Most often they were young men between twenty and thirty years of age. The corpses were thrown together in piles, and when there were enough of them, they were taken away on a truck and buried in a big common grave. It often smelled terrible, because in Porta we didn't have any crematorium. The camp was not big enough for that."[8]

More than half of the Danish prisoners in Porta Concentration Camp were to die by the day of the camp's liberation, March 20, 1945. Kiær claims that his own survival was due only to his strong desire to get back to his family.

About the time Kiær was captured, in March 1944, Juhl drove into a Danish garage in his huge Adler limousine. His automobile needed some minor repairs. The mechanic said that they would take about an hour. Juhl and his driver decided to spend the hour drinking beer in a nearby cafe. No

sooner were the Nazis gone than the mechanic, a member of
the Elsinore Sewing Club, started examining all of the papers
he could find in the automobile. One was a large map of
Snekkersten with crosses marking four houses—Snekkersten
Inn, two houses of fishermen involved in refugee transportation and Dr. Gersfelt's home. This information was quickly
passed on to those concerned. Dr. Gersfelt went into hiding,
but Thomsen decided to remain at the inn.

When no raid took place after several weeks, Gersfelt felt
that it was safe to go back to his own quarters. Several nights
after they had moved back to their house, Gersfelt and his
wife were awakened at three o'clock in the morning by
pounding on their front door. They feared it was the Gestapo, but, when Gersfelt opened the door, he saw that it was
Thomsen. The innkeeper was without overcoat or hat, and
soaking wet from the cold rain. He had just overheard a
Gestapo officer telling a girl at the inn that there would be a
raid on Snekkersten the following day, and had come to warn
Gersfelt. Once more the physician and his wife, now in her
ninth month of pregnancy, went into hiding.

What Thomsen had overheard was correct. It was unfortunate, however, that Thomsen had not been able to over-
hear further details of the planned raid. If he had, he might
have learned that its primary target was to be his own inn.
While Gersfelt was able to go into hiding and, several days
later, to flee to Sweden, Thomsen was seized by the Germans,
tortured and later executed.

The work of the Elsinore Sewing Club was at an end.

Chapter *13* FERRYING SERVICE

I am for those that have never been master'd
For men and women whose tempers have never been
master'd
For those whom laws, theories, conventions can never
master . . .

—WALT WHITMAN

IN OCTOBER 1943, Ole Helweg, a young Danish architect, was living and working in Sweden.[1] He had a good job and had recently married a young Swedish girl who was, even by Swedish standards, an outstanding beauty. He gave virtually no thought to the war or the German occupation of his country until he heard on the Swedish radio of the German persecution of the Danish Jews. He told his wife that even if it meant quitting his job and endangering his life by going back to Denmark, he had to do something to help his fellow countrymen of the Jewish faith. She agreed.

Helweg contacted another Danish architect living in Sweden at the time, Bent Karlby, and the two of them went to Stockholm, where they met with Ebbe Munch, head of the Swedish branch of the Danish underground. They told Munch that they wanted to quit their jobs and work full time ferrying Jews from Denmark to Sweden.

"It's fine that you want to help transport the Jewish refugees," said Munch, "but first you need money for a boat, and,
secondly, you need someone with seagoing experience."

Munch suggested that they try to get money from some of
the wealthy Jews in Stockholm, but could not think immediately of any possible seagoing assistants. The first Swedish
Jews Helweg and Karlby contacted were the Hollanders, well-
known Stockholm furriers. When Helweg told them the reason he needed money, they immediately handed him thirty-
five thousand dollars in cash, demanding no receipt and making
no conditions.

The next step was to get someone with seagoing experience.
Karlby had heard about a Danish navy lieutenant by the name
of Erik Stærmose who had fled to Sweden after scuttling the
ship on which he had served. They traced him to a sleazy hotel
room where he was holed up with no money and nothing to
do. He leaped at the opportunity to join them, recommending
a fourth man for the group—Erik Marx, a German Jewish
refugee who had escaped from a Nazi concentration camp and
who had been living for the past several months in Sweden,
where he had been working as a fisherman. When Helweg
and Karlby met Marx they saw that in looks and speech he
could easily pass for a Swede, and accepted him into the group.
In Göteborg, they purchased two boats, a 300-horsepower
Chris-Craft capable of going 40 knots an hour and of holding
ten passengers, and a fishing boat which was considerably
slower but capable of holding more passengers. They planned
to use the Chris-Craft in lighter weather and the fishing boat
in heavier seas. With boats and men to run them, they felt ready
for action and reported back to Ebbe Munch in Stockholm,
who gave them their official underground name of "Danish-
Swedish Refugee Service." Unofficially they referred to themselves simply as "The Ferrying Service." Munch informed
them that the Gestapo was now out in force in the towns north
of Copenhagen, such as Elsinore, Snekkersten, Gilleleje and

Humlebæk, and suggested that their unit operate south of Copenhagen from small fishing villages such as Klintholm and Møen. The trip across the sound would be considerably longer but, thought Munch, safer. The Ferrying Service agreed.[2]

Both boats were shipped by train to Malmø, which, after consultation with Munch, they decided to make their point of operation from Sweden. However, upon arrival in Malmø they discovered that the Swedish Intelligence Service had found out about their organization, and had put all four of them under surveillance, forbidding them to leave with either boat for Denmark. Helweg's wife had relatives in the Swedish Foreign Ministry, and through them Helweg was able to arrange an appointment to see Swedish Foreign Minister Christian Günther. He did not quite know what he could expect from Günther in the way of help, because Günther had a reputation as a pro-Nazi, based largely upon his decision earlier in the war to allow German troops to pass through Sweden on their way to Norway. However, Germany no longer seemed likely to win the war, and Helweg thought that there was a possibility that the Foreign Minister might now see things in a different light. Much to Helweg's gratification, Günther agreed to help him. He ordered the police surveillance dropped, gave Helweg's boats special permissions to sail in and out of Malmø Harbor at will, supplied Helweg and his friends with official documents identifying them as Swedish fishermen and guaranteed all the gasoline needed from Swedish Air Force supplies.

On the night of October 10, 1943, the Danish-Swedish Refugee Service set out from Malmø on its first trip. The destination was Copenhagen, and on board the fishing boat was its first passenger, Leif B. Hendil, an important underground leader, who was returning to Denmark from Sweden.[3] As luck would have it, several hours out of Malmø a violent storm developed which stopped the engine of the fishing boat. After drifting for hours, they were picked up by a Danish fishing boat. With the aid of the fishermen, they managed to get the engine started again. However, there still seemed something wrong with it, and, rather than take a chance on trying to make it to Copenhagen, Karlby decided to take the boat back to Malmø to be fixed, while Helweg and Hendil went on to Copenhagen with the fishermen who had picked them up. Several hours later, as the boat tied up at the Copenhagen docks, Helweg and Hendil, posing as fishermen, immediately started yelling, "Fish for sale! Fish for sale!" They sold over a hundred dollars' worth of fish for the fishermen who had saved them, and then, thinking that this was at least a token repayment, disappeared into the crowd.

Helweg's purpose in coming to Copenhagen, in addition to transporting Hendil, was to make contacts in the small towns south of Copenhagen designated by Munch. Among those he contacted were Werner Christiansen, owner of an inn at Rødvig, and Edvard Tesdorpf, owner of an enormous estate at Gjørslev, south of Copenhagen. Christiansen agreed to let Helweg use his inn, and Tesdorpf agreed to let Helweg use the beach on his estate, as pickup points for the refugees. In addition, contacts were established at Klintholm and Møen. All of this was arranged in a matter of days. Helweg returned to Denmark and the work of the Danish-Swedish Refugee Service began in earnest. At the beginning it went remarkably well.

Among the refugees picked up at Møen was the family of Ettie Henriques.[4] They were farmers, and their farm was located about 50 miles south of Copenhagen. When they were first contacted by the local police chief and told of the necessity of their escaping to Sweden, they were reluctant to take any action. Descendants of one of the oldest and most respected Jewish families in Denmark—their ancestors had arrived in the early part of the seventeenth century—they could not believe that after three centuries of acceptance and liberty it was necessary for them to flee what they had long considered their native land in order to save their lives. After continued

warnings by the police chief and, finally, contact by the underground, they agreed to go to Sweden via the Danish-Swedish
Refugee Service. Because of the severe gasoline rationing in
effect at the time, Ettie Henriques, then in her early twenties,
went with her family to the cliffs at Møen in a horse-drawn
cart. At the rendezvous they met a group of about forty other
refugees of various ages and from different parts of the country. Under the direction of an underground agent, the difficult
descent down the steep cliffs began. When they were about a
quarter of the way down, an airplane appeared, and the refugees, thinking it was a German plane which might open fire on
them, were seized by panic. They climbed back up the cliffs
and fled into the woods.

"It was awful," explained Ettie Henriques. "Old people,
children, mothers and fathers carrying babies, all fleeing every
which way into the woods."

Patiently, the underground gathered them all together
again, and the next day they were able to descend the cliffs and
board Stærmose's fishing boat, which took them to Malmø
without incident.

Because of the difficulty in climbing down the cliffs encountered by many of the refugees, especially the older ones
and those carrying infants, the pickup point at Møen was
dropped.

As the underground became better organized in working
with the various groups that had developed escape routes for
the refugees, Jews were transported from Copenhagen and the
northern towns to the southern areas where they could be
picked up by the Danish-Swedish Refugee Service.

The Tesdorpf estate proved particularly valuable as a contact point. The underground felt that Edvard Tesdorpf, a de-
scendant of one of the oldest and wealthiest aristocratic families
in Denmark, could not possibly be suspected by the Germans
as being a party to a rescue operation of the Jews. Actually,
he had become involved by accident. Returning home to the

estate one evening, he was told by his wife that there would be a dozen guests for dinner.

"Who are they?" he asked.

"I don't know," she replied matter-of-factly. "The only thing I know about them is that they're Jews fleeing arrest by the Germans. They simply turned up at the estate earlier this afternoon and asked if I would hide them. Naturally, I couldn't turn them away!"[5]

"Of course," replied her husband. "We must do everything we can to help them."

From that day on, word spread that the Tesdorpfs could be counted on as friends of the Jews, and increasingly large numbers of them began showing up at the estate daily. After contact by Helweg, Tesdorpf readily agreed to make the estate not only a hiding place, but a major pickup point in the area.

"Actually, it was all rather exciting," explained Mrs. Tesdorpf. "Every time we took the refugees down to the beach on our estate where they were to meet one of the boats I kept hearing over and over in my head 'The Smuggler's Theme' from *Carmen*."

After transporting over seven hundred Jews to Sweden, Helweg, Stærmose, Marx and Karlby continued their Ferrying Service for the benefit of saboteurs, downed Allied airmen and any others who, for one reason or another, had to get to Sweden or had to be smuggled from Sweden into Denmark. In addition, they transported mail, arms, ammunition and secret photographs and films of German fortifications.

On the night of December 10, 1944, Helweg, Stærmose and Marx were transporting a shipment of arms to the underground in Denmark. They were in their fishing boat on the way to Copenhagen from Malmø when they were spotted by a German patrol boat and ordered to halt. Before the patrol boat came alongside, they were able to throw overboard all of the submachine guns, pistols and hand grenades they were carrying. They had false papers showing that they were

Swedish fishermen, but, in addition, they had the Danish identification papers which they needed in Denmark. After the Germans boarded their boat and placed them under arrest on grounds of suspicion, Helweg asked if he and Stærmose could have permission to urinate over the side of the boat. Permission was granted. While urinating, they ate their Danish identification papers. Helweg knew that he and Marx could pass for Swedes, but that Stærmose could not, because he spoke practically no Swedish. "Don't talk," whispered Helweg to Stærmose. "Never talk. Pretend that you're an idiot. Dementia praecox." A few minutes later Marx asked for permission to relieve himself over the side of the boat, and, while doing so, he too ate his Danish identification papers.

For the next twelve days, Helweg, Stærmose and Marx were kept in Vestre Prison in Copenhagen. Stærmose not only maintained an absolute silence, but kept a blank look on his face. Fortunately, he shared the same cell with Helweg, and since Helweg's father was a psychiatrist, Helweg was able to coach him on what someone suffering from a severe case of dementia praecox looked like.

One day a Gestapo officer asked Helweg, "Why do you keep that big oaf? He's abnormal."

"Yes," replied Helweg, "there's no doubt that he's mentally unbalanced, but he is enormously strong. Look at his hands. Did you ever see such big hands? He is very helpful to us."

All during their questioning by the Gestapo, Helweg and Marx maintained that they were Swedish fishermen and had absolutely no idea why they were under suspicion by the Germans.

Finally the Gestapo announced that they were convinced that the three of them were Swedish fishermen and that they were going to give them their freedom. Before their release, they were called in for a final questioning.

"We're going to let you go because you're Swedish and Sweden is a neutral country," said the Gestapo officer in charge.

"However, I want you to remember that we are not obliged to free citizens of a neutral country if they have been engaged in illegal activities with the Danes. Do you understand that?"

Helweg and Marx nodded. Stærmose maintained his blank look.

"As a matter of fact," said the Gestapo officer, "we are absolutely positive that you have been engaged in illegal activities with the Danes. Nevertheless, we are going to let you go. Can you guess why?"

Helweg and Marx shook their heads. Stærmose remained motionless.

"Don't be so naïve," said the officer. "We have strong reason to suspect that you have been smuggling Jews into Sweden."

Much to Helweg's and Stærmose's surprise, Erik Marx suddenly spoke up. "As a matter of fact we have," he said.

"But why?" asked the Gestapo officer, looking at Marx. "You, especially, a blond, blue-eyed Swede, a perfect Aryan. Why would you want to help the Jews?"

Marx took a huge roll of bills out of his pocket and showed it to the Gestapo officer. "Here's why," he said. "For money."

"If it's money you want," said the Gestapo officer, "we'll pay you if you bring the refugees to us instead of to Sweden. Next time you get a batch of refugees, let us know. We'll pay you for them. In fact, that is the reason that we have decided to let you go. So you can bring the Jews to us instead of to Sweden—for money, of course."

"But we'll only be able to do it once," sad Marx. "Once and that'll be the end of it, because the refugees won't trust us again. Information, however, is a different story. Would you be willing to pay for information? In the end that may prove more valuable to you than handing over a boatload of refugees."

The Gestapo officer asked them to sit down. He offered them whiskey and cigarettes and told them to make themselves comfortable until he returned. He explained that he was going to call in some of his colleagues to meet with them. While they were alone, Marx explained to Helweg and Stærmose what he had in mind.

The Gestapo officer returned with several high-ranking superiors. A friendly discussion followed, in which Helweg and Marx agreed to act as double agents provided they got open permits from the Gestapo enabling them to have freedom of operation in any Danish port along the coast. The Gestapo agreed to this, and the following day they received their open permits and left the prison for their boat.

Naturally, they never lived up to their part of the agreement. Instead of cooperating with the Germans as they had promised, the Danish-Swedish Refugee Service used the open permits to operate with greater freedom for the remainder of the war.

Chapter *14* THE SHOOTING PRIEST

Notwithstanding our separate religious beliefs we will
fight to preserve for our Jewish brothers and sisters
the same freedom we ourselves value more than life.
                    —DANISH BISHOPS' PROCLAMATION,
                         October 3, 1943

RANDERS IS A TOWN of 50,000 in northern Jutland, about 193 miles northwest of Copenhagen. In 1943 its
Jewish population was, as it is now, about twenty. That all of
them arrived safely in Sweden is due in large measure to the
efforts of Pastor Poul Borchsenius, nicknamed by the Germans
"The Shooting Priest."[1]

On the day Denmark fell, Pastor Borchsenius was in his
house getting dressed in preparation for conducting the early-
morning service at his church. When he heard the roar of airplanes overhead, he went outside and looked up at the sky.
He was delighted by what he saw. Have we really so many
planes, he wondered? It was most reassuring. Then suddenly
one of the planes flew low and the pastor noticed the swas-
tika painted on its wing. This confused him. He telephoned
a friend, a colonel at the local Army garrison, who told him
that Denmark had been invaded by the Germans. Pastor

177

Borchsenius was stunned. Later that afternoon the German troops entered Randers. Borchsenius was on the street to greet them. Well over six feet tall, with the build of an athlete and the bald head of a Buddha, Borchsenius could not help but be noticed as he turned his back on the German soldiers as they marched by. The townspeople around him followed suit. During the next few weeks of the German occupation, the people of Randers, under Borchsenius' guidance, did something even more insulting than turning their backs to the Germans. Whenever they encountered German troops, they ignored them completely, pretending neither to see nor hear them, looking through them as though they were glass. It was obvious to Pastor Borchsenius, that this manifestation by the townspeople of their complete contempt for the Germans piqued them enormously. Nevertheless, the Germans took no reprisal measures against the social boycott. On the contrary, they not only continued to behave properly, but extended themselves to try to win over the inhabitants of Randers. It was to no avail. September 29 was the seventieth birthday of the King. Disobeying German orders, the population of Randers celebrated it by holding mass meetings, conducting mass walks along the town's main avenues and filling the air with patriotic Danish songs.

At the beginning of 1941 Pastor Borchsenius attended an affair celebrating the twenty-fifth anniversary of the Whitestone Inn, a resort hostelry six miles north of Randers. During the party, a newspaperman by the name of Kaj Holbeck invited Pastor Borchsenius for a walk outside. For the next several hours the newspaperman and the pastor strolled leisurely through the woods surrounding the Inn. Holbeck was obviously trying to size up Borchsenius by eliciting the pastor's opinions on a number of political matters.

"What is the point of all this?" asked Borchsenius.

"The Whitestone Inn," said Holbeck, "is the headquarters for an underground cell of which I am in charge. We use it as a hiding place and transfer point for saboteurs."

"Why are you telling this to me?"

"Because we would like you to become a member of our organization. You could help hide the saboteurs in your home or even in the church. As the towr's leading minister, I don't think the Germans would ever suspect you."

Borchsenius was flattered to be taken into Holbeck's confidence and delighted to be able to join the group and thus become one of Denmark's earliest resistance fighters.

When the Germans decided to arrest Denmark's Jews, it was only natural for Borchsenius to become involved in the rescue of the small number of Jews—mainly doctors and civil servants—in Randers. There was little difficulty and no real danger in getting the refugees across the sound to Sweden, but there were some incidents which proved particularly memorable to Pastor Borchsenius. At one time a Jewish police inspector from a nearby town came to see Borchsenius at his church. After the pastor assured him that he could get him safely to Sweden, the police inspector threw himself on the ground at Borchsenius' feet and shouted, "Why must I give up my job and my home and flee with my family to another country? Just because I happen to be born a Jew?" He lay on the floor crying. For a moment Pastor Borchsenius felt like offering him some words of consolation, but he realized that there was nothing to say. All he could do was to let him continue crying, and then, when he had stopped, to give him some sleeping tablets.

One amusing incident occurred as the result of the romantic involvement of a saboteur. The saboteur had been hiding in Pastor Borchsenius' home for several months, and, although wanted by the Germans and warned by the underground to remain indoors at all times, he would sneak out of the Pastor's house at night to look for girls. During his carousings he encountered one particular girl with whom he fell in love. He told Pastor Borchsenius that they had decided they wanted to marry before he was smuggled to Sweden, and wanted Borchsenius not only to perform the wedding ceremony, but to arrange a formal wedding dinner to which he and his fiancée could invite their relatives and friends. The pastor agreed to perform the ceremony, but told the saboteur that because of the strict rationing in effect, it would be impossible to provide the formal wedding dinner. The saboteur was deeply disappointed. A few days before the wedding ceremony was to take place— it was the second week of October 1943—Borchsenius was visited by the proprietor of the local cabaret. He asked the pastor if he would help smuggle out of the country two Jewish music-hall artists who had been performing at his cabaret. Borchsenius offered the cabaret-owner a proposition. He would help get "The Juggling Diamonts" to Sweden if, in return, the cabaret-owner would provide the wedding dinner of the saboteur. The cabaret-owner not only agreed, but offered his cabaret as the place to hold the wedding dinner. Several days after the saboteur and his bride were married and had their formal wedding dinner, the saboteur, together with "The Juggling Diamonts," was taken by fishing boat to Sweden.

In November, the resistance movement in Denmark began in earnest, and the underground group to which Pastor Borchsenius belonged received orders from the Free Denmark Council in London to try to break the railroad connections between Germany and Norway. This meant blowing up the railroad lines in Jutland, one of the main routes used by the Germans to and from Norway. Operating under his underground name "Hans Hansen," Pastor Borchsenius became one of the leading saboteurs of this group. It was at this time that the Germans nicknamed him "The Shooting Priest" and a price was put on his head.

On December 7, the underground decided that it had become too dangerous for Pastor Borchsenius to remain in Denmark. He, his wife and two daughters were ordered to Sweden. When he arrived in the town of Dragør, near Kastrup, he was told by the underground contact that two ships were leaving the following day. One was considered a "safe" ship, and the other "unsafe." Because the "safe" ship was full, Pastor Borchsenius and his family could either sail on the "unsafe" one, or wait several days for another ship. The pastor decided to take a chance on the "unsafe" ship. The following day they were led below deck, where they were crowded so close to the other passengers that it was impossible to move. To fit into the hold of the ship, all of the refugees had to sit on the floor with their knees pressed tightly against their chests. The crossing over took several hours and the boat rocked a great deal. Practically all of the passengers became seasick. Unable to move, Pastor Borchsenius could not avert the violently ill woman opposite him.

"I'm sorry, Pastor," said the woman, "but what can I do?"

"Nothing but what you're doing," said the pastor, bracing himself.

They finally reached Sweden, where several days later Pastor Borchsenius learned that the faster "safe" ship had been captured by the Germans and its passengers sent to Theresienstadt.

When asked why he helped the Jews, Pastor Borchsenius replied, "I can't tell you. Of course, I helped them, but I can't tell you why. It was spontaneous. Yes, all over the country it was spontaneous."

Chapter 15 TWO WOMEN

We have lived under the Dannebrog—*with its white cross that is the token of peace on a flaming field of blood. And now abide these three—faith, hope and love; but the greatest of them is love.*

—CHRISTIAN ULRIC HANSEN,
Danish patriot executed by
the Germans, June 23, 1944

IN THE TOWN OF DRAGØR, about eight miles south of Copenhagen, lived two women of widely disparate professions who were destined to become close friends because of a common interest: rescuing Danish Jews. They were Mrs. Ellen Nielsen, a fishmonger, and Miss Elise Schmidt-Petersen, a schoolteacher.

In 1941, Mrs. Nielsen's husband, a worker in a chemical factory, died. To support her six children, Mrs. Nielsen became a fishmonger on the Copenhagen docks, buying fish directly from the fishermen and hawking it to passers-by. She had no interest in politics.

During the first week of October 1943, while she was hawking fish on the docks, she was approached by two brothers. They were flower-vendors in the flower market adjacent to the fish market, and she knew them only because they would occasionally buy fish from her, and she, in turn, would sometimes purchase flowers from them.

"What will you have today, boys?" she asked. "The cod is very nice and I have some fresh shrimp."[1]

"Mrs. Nielsen, we wonder if you could help us," said one of the brothers. "You know many fishermen. Perhaps you know one who would be willing to take us to Sweden. We would pay him two thousand kroner to take us across."

"But why would you want to do that?" asked Mrs. Nielsen.

"Because we are Jewish, and the Germans have started arresting all Danish Jews."

This was the first knowledge Mrs. Nielsen had of the brothers being Jewish and the first she had heard of the German roundup of the Jews.

"But if the Germans are arresting the Jews, what are you boys doing walking around here? Shouldn't you be in hiding?"

"Yes, but we don't know where to hide," replied one of the brothers.

"You can stay at my house," said Mrs. Nielsen. "I'll close early today and you can come home with me. And while you're in my house, I'll ask among the fishermen I know whether any of them would be willing to take you to Sweden."

During the next few days, Mrs. Nielsen managed to find several fishermen willing to take the brothers to Sweden. Arrangements were made with one of them, and the flower-vendors were taken safely across the sound. Through the fisherman who had taken them, word reached the underground of what Mrs. Nielsen had done, and they contacted her to ask whether she would be willing to aid more refugees to escape from the Germans. Because her work put her in direct contact with the fishermen on the docks, she was in a position to be a perfect liaison between them and the underground. Mrs. Nielsen agreed to do what she could and during the following weeks over a hundred refugees passed through her house on their way to Sweden. At one time, Mrs. Nielsen had over thirty refugees squeezed into her small house. Her children aided her in her work by helping to feed and care for the refugees, and, in addition, her two eldest sons acted as guides, leading the refugees from the house to the boats in the harbor. After the refugees were safe in Sweden, Mrs. Nielsen continued to work for the underground by hiding saboteurs.

In December 1944, Mrs. Nielsen was caught by the Gestapo. For three months she was in Vestre Prison, where the Gestapo tried unsuccessfully to get her to reveal the names of her contacts. She was then sent to Frøslev Concentration Camp for another three months, and from there to Ravensbrück in Germany. Upon her arrival in Ravensbrück, she was summoned to the office of the camp commandant.

"Mrs. Nielsen," said the commandant, "we know that you have been involved in the illegal transportation of Jews from Denmark to Sweden."

Mrs. Nielsen remained silent.

"There is no point in denying it," said the commandant, "because we have proof. We know, for example, that you saved the lives of dozens of Jewish children. We even have some of their names."

There was no reply from Mrs. Nielsen.

"No matter," continued the commandant. "The point is that we feel that since you were involved with the transportation of Jewish children in Denmark, we should give you a job here in Ravensbrück that would use to advantage your previous experience and interests. We are therefore giving you a job similar to the one you had in Denmark—transporting Jewish children."

Mrs. Nielsen had no idea what the commandant meant. But she learned all too soon. Her assignment was to carry those Jewish infants too young to walk to the gas chambers where they were put to death. She was also made to carry them, after they were gassed, to the crematorium to be burned. When, after several weeks, she refused to continue at her macabre job, she was condemned to death, and she was herself placed three times on the line leading to the gas chamber. The first time she saved herself by bribing a guard with a bar of soap which she had received in a Danish Red Cross parcel. The second time she was able to do the same with the contents of another Danish parcel. The third time she had nothing left with which to bribe the guards. Waiting on the line, stripped naked, she was resigned to death. Suddenly she was approached by German guards who informed her that she had been saved.

Count Folke Bernadotte had made an agreement with Heinrich Himmler to have all surviving Danish concentration camp prisoners shipped to Sweden for internment.

Working closely with Mrs. Nielsen in hiding Jewish refugees in Dragør was her neighbor, Miss Elise Schmidt-Petersen, a schoolteacher. Like Mrs. Nielsen, Miss Petersen offered no opposition to the Germans until the start of the Jewish persecution. The extent of her political naïveté is shown by her reactions on the day of the German occupation. She was bicycling from her home in Dragør to her school in Copenhagen when she met a friend on the road who told her that the turnoff ahead was blocked because German planes were landing at nearby Kastrup Airport.

"What does that mean?" asked Miss Petersen.[2]

"It means that the Germans have taken over the country."

Miss Petersen turned her bicycle around to take an alternate route to the school. She had no idea whether Germany's taking over the country was good or bad for Denmark. She would inquire, she thought, when she arrived at the school and spoke to some of the teachers. At the school the teachers were divided in their reaction to the German occupation. Very few were violently opposed to it. The general feeling was that, good or bad, nothing could be done about it.

During the second week of October 1943, Miss Petersen

received a telephone call from Kaj Holbeck, the newspaper editor who had first introduced Pastor Poul Borchsenius to resistance activities. Miss Petersen had worked for Holbeck as a housemaid when she was a young girl, and, since becoming a teacher, had often asked Holbeck to visit her in Dragør. During the war years, Holbeck had consistently claimed that he was too busy to visit her, but she never pressed the issue because she knew from mutual friends the reason—he was one of the leaders of the underground.

"Is your invitation for me to come up to have tea with you still good?" asked Holbeck.

"Yes, of course," replied Miss Petersen. "When would you like to come?"

"Tonight. And, if it is all right with you, I would like to bring seven guests with me. I hope that you will have enough tea for all of us. Is it all right?"

Miss Petersen knew that if she answered in the affirmative it would mean getting involved in some sort of underground activity. "Yes," she replied, "of course you can come. And by all means bring your guests."

Holbeck's seven guests were Danish Jews. Among them was a six-month-old girl and two boys of eight and ten years of age. Holbeck explained that they were leaving that night, after midnight, from Dragør for Sweden. Miss Petersen offered them food and tea, but they were all too nervous to eat. The two young boys were particularly upset.

"Why must we keep waiting?" asked the ten-year-old. "Why can't we go now?"

"We must wait for a man to come and take us to the boat," explained the father.

"Can't you telephone this man?" asked the son.

"What should I tell him if I telephone him?"

"Tell him to come and take us now," said the son. "Tell him we can't wait any longer. Please."

Miss Petersen spoke to the boy and told him not to be afraid,

that he would soon be in Sweden. Seeing how frightened the
two boys were, seeing the terror of the baby's mother, Miss
Petersen was glad that she had agreed to help Holbeck. She
turned to him and said, "You can use my house for this type of
thing any time you wish to."

At midnight a doctor arrived at the house and told them that
their boat was ready, that they would soon be boarding it, and
that, meanwhile, it was his job to administer injections to the
three children. The children received the injections, and Miss
Petersen, watching them become unconscious, found the sight
almost more than she could bear. A few minutes after the
doctor departed, there was a knock on the door. When Miss
Petersen opened it, she was frightened to see standing in the
doorway a Danish policeman. He quickly explained that he
was a member of the resistance and that he had come to lead
the refugees to the boat. The three unconscious children were
wrapped in rugs and carried down to the harbor.

After the seven refugees were safely on their way to Sweden,
Holbeck asked Miss Petersen, "Did you mean what you said a
little while ago about using your house any time we wanted to?"

"Yes," answered Miss Petersen. "Of course I meant it."

Miss Petersen's house in Dragør was tiny—two small rooms
and a kitchen—but during the next few weeks she managed to
hide over fifty refugees in it. She worked very closely with
Mrs. Nielsen in this operation, often receiving the overflow
from Mrs. Nielsen's house. Some of the refugees were hidden
in her house for a few hours, but several stayed for as many as
three or four days at a time. She housed one particular group of
refugees for ten days. The underground supplied her with
ration cards, but the money with which she purchased the food
for the refugees was her own. "Money meant nothing when
you had to help people at a time like that," explained Miss
Petersen.

After the exodus of the refugees, she continued to work
closely with Mrs. Nielsen in the hiding and transporting of

saboteurs. One of the first of the saboteurs to be hidden in her house was Pastor Borchsenius.

In August 1944, Miss Petersen's role in the underground was discovered, and she had to go into hiding herself. Using a fictitious name and false identity papers, she moved from one friend's house to another until the end of the war.

Why did Miss Petersen help the Jews? "I thought it was my duty," she said.

Chapter 16 THE WINE MERCHANT

There exists in each of us a tremendous force, if we know how to use it, for the victims of human oppression.

—GEORGES CLEMENCEAU

THROUGHOUT DENMARK the people cooperated with underground units to ferry the Jews safely to Sweden. In and around Copenhagen, the main organized groups were Mogens Staffeldt's bookshop, Bispebjerg Hospital, the Rockefeller Institute and "the house with the blue curtains" at Lyngby. In the North, the Elsinore Sewing Club comprised the main underground unit. The Danish-Swedish Refugee Service operated in the South. In addition, there were hundreds of refugees, especially in the early days of the flight, who got to Sweden by making their arrangements with fishermen independently. But no matter how the Jews finally arrived in Sweden, there is no doubt that very few of them would have succeeded without the eager and full-hearted cooperation of the entire Danish population.

The unique escape of Benjamin Slor, a wine merchant, illustrates the importance of the average Dane in the total rescue operation of the Jews.[1]

Slor had come to Denmark from Palestine shortly after World War I to become a gym teacher. He had worked his way through Europe by a series of menial jobs and, when he finally arrived in Copenhagen for his interview at the school to which he had applied for admission, his clothes were ragged. He made sure to leave his shabby coat in the anteroom before going into the headmaster's office. Picking up the coat after the interview, he found that two missing buttons had been replaced by new ones and the coat itself had been brushed clean and pressed. When he expressed his astonishment, the headmaster's daughter told him that while he had been talking to her father, she had taken it upon herself to sew and clean his coat. "I was so moved by that," explained Slor, "that I said to myself that this must be not only a wonderful place to study but a wonderful country in which to settle down and live." And this is exactly what Slor did. Completing his studies, he married a Swedish girl and he and his wife started to raise a family. Instead of becoming a gym teacher, he opened a wineshop specializing in imports from Palestine. Active in the Jewish community of Copenhagen, Slor quickly became renowned for his charm and warm humor. He temporarily lost that sense of humor, when the Germans invaded Denmark. Having spent time in Germany while on his way to Denmark, he knew the Germans' character and greatly feared their potential cruelty, particularly toward the Jews. He was concerned not only for the safety of his own family, but for that of several hundred young Jewish refugees from Germany and Poland who were training as *chaluzim* in Denmark. Together with Julius Margolinsky, he was the organizer of their training program. As the days following the invasion went by, it seemed to Slor, as it did to the entire Jewish population of Denmark, that the Germans had no intention of introducing any anti-Jewish measures in the country. Slor abandoned plans for his wife and family to go to Sweden, and encouraged the *chaluzim* to continue their training in the open. His sense of humor returned, and, to see how far the Germans would go in their permissive attitude toward the Jews, Slor began setting up in his store obvious displays of wine jugs from Palestine. When his brother-in-law saw the displays, he reprimanded Slor.

"Why look for trouble?" asked the brother-in-law.

"I want to see if I can irritate them," said Slor. "Maybe if I irritate them enough, they won't come in here and I won't have to do any business with them."

"Maybe if you irritate them enough," said the nervous brother-in-law, "they'll arrest you and send you to a German concentration camp."

Pursuing his own devilish instincts, Slor set up the displays. The following afternoon several German soldiers entered the store and one of them asked Slor about the odd lettering on the jugs.

"That's Hebrew," replied Slor.

"Where do they come from?" asked the soldier.

"From Palestine," replied Slor, "the same place I come from."

The soldier showed no shock, no surprise. All he said was, "Isn't that interesting!" He then bought two bottles of French wine and, together with his companions, departed. He and other German soldiers made quite a few visits to Slor's store during the next few years, but, until 1943, their only purpose was to buy wine.

On October 2, Slor's wife, having been born in Sweden, was able to enter Sweden legally from Denmark together with her two children. That evening, Slor was contacted by his friend Vilhelm Leifer, a Danish police officer who served as liaison between the Danes and the Germans.

"You've got to get to Sweden as soon as possible," said Leifer. "The Germans know all about you. They know about your trips to Palestine, about your contacts with Jewish officials there. You are the one Jew they most want to pick up."

"Leave for Sweden?" said Slor. "Easier said than done. My wife could leave because she's Swedish, but I . . ."

"You can leave tomorrow," said Leifer. "I've already made arrangements with the underground."

"No, I can't," said Slor. "I can't leave until I take care of my *chaluzim.*"

"You're as stubborn as Margolinsky," said Leifer. "He, too, won't leave because he's worried about his precious *chaluzim.*"

"Good for him," said Slor.

For the next six weeks Benjamin Slor lived the life of a fugitive. He never slept twice in the same place. Nightly he moved to a different quarter of the city. He had a wide choice of hideouts. Each night four or five different Christian friends volunteered to hide him. It was in vain, however, that Slor attempted to speak to the *chaluzim,* who were hidden on farms in Jutland. The farmers who protected them were afraid of spies. They knew Slor by name, but had no way of knowing that it was truly Slor who was now calling them on the telephone. Whenever Slor telephoned and asked to speak to the *chaluzim,* the farmers replied that they didn't know what he was talking about. Slor knew that it would be impossible to travel to Jutland to help the *chaluzim* directly, but he felt that their knowing that he was still in Denmark would at least be an aid to their morale. And so, whenever he telephoned and a farmer feigned ignorance of the subject, Slor would say, "Well, anyway, tell them Slor telephoned to tell them not to worry. We'll get them out of the country somehow."

Through his efforts, the *chaluzim* found out about his continued presence in Denmark and it was undoubtedly a source of consolation to them. At the same time, however, the Germans discovered that he was still around, and they redoubled their efforts to catch him. A price was put on his head and *Fædrelandet,* a Nazi newspaper published in Denmark, printed a large photograph of Slor on its front page. Over it ran the headline: "LITTLE BENJAMIN, THE AX IS READY TO FALL!"

By the middle of November, Leifer was able to inform Slor that the Danish underground had gotten all of the *chaluzim* safely to Sweden. "You yourself simply must get out of the country now," Leifer told him. "You are a menace not only to yourself but to the various underground groups with which you've had contact. I've been told to tell you that if you're not out of the country within two or three days, the underground will not be responsible for what happens to you."

"All right," said Slor. "If the *chaluzim* are all in Sweden, I suppose that I can go there, too."

He was sent into hiding at a villa in Klampenborg, a suburb about six miles north of Copenhagen, and ordered to remain indoors until further contact by the underground. After four days in the villa, Slor felt the need to stretch his limbs and, donning workman's clothes, went into the garden. He had trimmed the shrubbery and was mowing the lawn when a Gestapo car pulled up on the grounds and several Gestapo officers jumped out.

"Hey, gardener," yelled one of them, "are there any Jews hiding in that villa?"

"There may be," replied Slor. "Why don't you take a look."

"Thank you," said the Gestapo officer, motioning his men toward the house. As they entered the house, Slor, not wanting to give them a second look at the face which had recently appeared on the front page of their newspaper, disappeared down the road. Returning to Copenhagen, he was hidden in the home of his friend Henri Smyth, a director of the Swedish-Orient Line. Several days later, he was contacted at Smyth's home by Leifer, who told him that arrangements had finally been made for his escape to Sweden. For details, he was to go, at exactly six that evening, to the Glyptoteket Restaurant opposite the Carlsberg Museum of Ancient Art. He was to sit at the bar and order two drinks—a whiskey and a cognac—and three spoons. He was to put one spoon in the cognac glass and two spoons in the whiskey glass, and wait for a man to come along who would be wearing a monocle and who would order a whiskey-cognac. This would be Slor's contact, and Slor would receive further instructions from him.

At 6 P.M. Slor entered the Glyptoteket Restaurant and, following Leifer's instructions, made contact with the man with a monocle.

"Are you Slor?"

"Yes. What is your name?"

"Never mind that. Are you ready to leave tonight?"

"No," replied Slor.

The man stared at Slor through his monocle. "Why not?"

"It will take me another day or two to contact my brother-in-law. He is still in Denmark and I want him to leave with me."

"It would be best for you to leave as soon as possible. Where can I reach you?"

Slor gave him Henri Smyth's address.

Two days later, Slor received a stern warning from the underground: whether or not he had managed to reach his brother-in-law, he had to leave for Sweden that evening. Fortunately, he had contacted his brother-in-law, who was eager and ready to leave with him. Before leaving, Slor and his brother-in-law were visited by the man with the monocle, who gave them their final instructions. These instructions seemed particularly odd and rather hazardous to Slor, but he promised to follow them, hoping that the underground knew what it was doing.

The first instruction was to take the midnight train to Berlin. This, the underground agent explained, was to throw the Germans off guard; they would never think of looking for Slor on a train on which most of the passengers were German troops returning home.

Midnight found Slor and his brother-in-law lost in a babble of German voices. Several other Danes were aboard the midnight special to Berlin, but most of the passengers were German soldiers and German civilian workers attached to the occupation forces. As the train pulled out of the station, a German officer sitting opposite Slor smiled and said, "Well, it won't be long now." Slor smiled back at him. Slor's brother-in-law developed a coughing jag which lasted for several minutes. The train rolled on toward the German border, and Slor wondered whether he and his brother-in-law would be able to carry out the second part of their instructions. Before they could do so, something had to happen over which they had no control—the train had to be wrecked.

Just before the town of Haarlev, in southern Zealand, about 25 miles south of Copenhagen, Slor and his brother were jolted out of their seats as the train came to a sudden halt. The word "sabotage" spread through the train, and Slor and his brother-in-law, following the instructions of the man with the monocle, stepped outside, along with many of the other passengers, "to have a look." The train was surrounded on both sides by heavy woods. Steam and smoke bellowed forth from the engine. Slor and his brother-in-law walked to the front of the engine, but, unlike the other passengers, they had little interest in it. What they were really interested in looking at were the woods on the left side of the tracks, where, they had been told, they would receive a special signal. In the darkness of the woods there suddenly appeared what they had been waiting for—two brief flashes of light, as if someone had very quickly turned a flashlight on and off twice. They waited several minutes for the signal to be repeated. It was. Then, when all eyes were on the engineer, who was screaming his head off at the fireman about the engine failure, they slipped into the woods on the left side of the tracks. If the signal had been a single flash of light, they would have entered the woods on the right side of the tracks.

Slor's instructions were to march straight ahead into the woods, but because it was so dark he had no idea whether they were walking in the right direction. After about twenty minutes, a flashlight beam fell upon them.

"Slor?"

"Yes."

A man stepped forward out of the darkness. "Valentin Rasmussen, beer salesman." They shook hands.

They followed the beer salesman for about half an hour until they came to his small house. Inside, Rasmussen introduced them to his wife, who had prepared a hot meal for them. Because they were exhausted from the tension of the trip, they asked to be excused from the meal, and wondered if they could go to sleep immediately. Rasmussen led them to their room, where they quickly undressed and got into bed. But they could not sleep. Although they could not make out the words, they were kept awake by violent quarreling between Rasmussen and his wife. Slor's brother-in-law was worried lest the wife, considering their presence in her house dangerous, might turn them in to the Gestapo. Slor was too exhausted to care or to try to think of anything to do about it. Eventually the arguing stopped and Slor and his brother-in-law fell asleep.

The next morning, over a hearty breakfast, Valentin Rasmussen asked Slor, "Did you hear us quarreling last night?"

"I seem to recall hearing some raised voices," said Slor, "but I was too tired to pay any attention to it."

"My wife was angry with me," said Rasmussen. "She said, 'You promised to bring me four Jews last night, but you brought only two.' You see, originally I was supposed to bring four. There were actually four of you on the train last night."

"What happened to the other two?" asked Slor.

"Oh, they are all right. Our plans were changed at the last minute, and they were taken to a doctor's house nearby."

From the cap and apron Rasmussen was wearing, Slor saw that he was a salesman for the Carlsberg Breweries.

"Do you have another Carlsberg cap and apron?" asked Slor.

"Yes, why?"

"If you lend it to me, I'll help you sell beer," said Slor.

"Are you crazy?" said his brother-in-law. "We're supposed to stay hidden in the house until it's time to go to the boat."

"You can stay in the house if you want to," replied Slor, "but I'll go mad if I have to stay cooped up."

For the next four days, disguised in a Carlsberg Beer cap and apron, Benjamin Slor helped Rasmussen load cases of beer onto his truck and deliver them to the local stores.

On the fifth night that Slor and his brother-in-law were at the Rasmussens' there was a loud pounding on the door which awakened the entire household. Rasmussen opened the door and let in three local townspeople from Haarlev—a doctor, a lawyer and a teacher. After talking to them briefly, he led them to Slor's room.

"One of the two Jews staying at the doctor's house is crying," said Rasmussen. "The doctor can't calm him down. Neither can the others. He has poison and threatens to take it. The doctor's wife is with him now. They thought that perhaps you could go with them and talk to the man."

Slor dressed and went with the three men to the doctor's house. The elderly Danish Jew was crying bitterly.

"I'd like to be alone with him," said Slor.

The others left the room and Slor sat on the edge of the man's bed. "Do you speak Yiddish?"

"Yes."

"What's the matter?" he asked in Yiddish.

"I'm afraid. I want to kill myself, but I haven't the courage."

"Why do you want to kill yourself?"

"It would be better than being taken by the Germans."

"But so far you haven't been taken by the Germans."

"But I'm afraid I will be. I don't understand it. Why should all of these people, complete strangers, want to help us? Maybe one of them will turn us in to the Germans."

"But they haven't yet."

"No, that's true."

"I'll make a bargain with you," said Slor. "Right now you're nervous and upset. You may do something rash. Look, we are in this together. We will be making the attempt to get to Sweden together. I give you my word of honor that if we are captured by the Germans, I'll return the poison to you."

The old man opened his clenched fist. Slor took the vial of poison out of his hand.

Several days later Slor was informed by Rasmussen that in a few hours he and his brother-in-law would be taken to a boat in Haarlev Harbor. A Lutheran pastor dropped by to give them his blessings. "*Shalom, Shalom!*" he said, then added, also in Hebrew, "May the Lord bless you and keep you." His last words to Slor were in Danish: "I pray that very soon we shall meet again here in Denmark—*our* land."

Slor, his brother-in-law and the two Danish Jews in hiding in the doctor's house were concealed in a cattle car. They were driven by a farmer they did not know to a small fishing boat in the harbor at Haarlev. A fisherman they did not know took them over to Sweden.

Chapter 17 THE CROSSING

> *Will it come, the hour of my freedom?*
> *Time, Time!—I call to it;*
> *I roam above the sea, I wait for the weather,*
> *I beckon to the sail of ships.*
>
> —PUSHKIN, *Evgenyi Onegin*

THERE ARE AS MANY escape stories as there were crossings, and there were over a thousand crossings. In some cases, it was a question of a few minutes in a fast speedboat. In other cases, it was a question of many hours in crowded, uncomfortable quarters.

When it became evident to the Germans that large numbers of Danish Jews were escaping to Sweden by boat, they used police dogs to try to sniff out the human cargo aboard the ships. To overcome this, a Danish scientist in Malmø concocted a powder made of dried human blood and cocaine which, when dusted on the decks of the ships, completely deadened the dogs' sense of smell. In addition, small amounts of it were placed in carefully folded handkerchiefs which were distributed to key Danish seamen. When the Germans came aboard the ships with their dogs, the seamen, pretending to blow their noses with their handkerchiefs, would let the light gray powder fall to the decks in the vicinity of the dogs. The simple chemical formula, dusted onto the decks or dropped from handkerchiefs, worked with astounding success. The Germans never found out why their highly trained police dogs were completely ineffective.

For the most part, the Danish Jews escaping to Sweden were transported in small fishing boats. Occasionally, as in the case of the trap-rock schooner owned by a Mexican skipper, larger vessels were used. In still other instances, even rowboats were sometimes used.

One Danish Jew, with his parents and an uncle and aunt, went to Humlebæk, where he hoped to be able to arrange for fishing-boat transportation that very evening.[1] Unfortunately, no boat was immediately available. Disappointed and discouraged, he and his family went from the docks to a restaurant, where they discussed the possibility of giving themselves up to the Germans. The son opposed the idea, pleading that they make another attempt the following night.

"But where can we go tonight?" asked the mother. "Who will hide us? We can't go on like this. I can't take it any longer." She buried her head in her arms and began to cry.

There were two young men at a nearby table observing the scene. One of them approached the distressed family.

"Are you people in trouble because of the Germans?" he asked.

"Yes," replied the son.

"Are you Jews?"

"Yes."

"If you're willing to take the chance, my friend and I will row you across to Sweden."

"When?"

"We have our own boat. We can leave right now."

Seven hours later they were in Sweden.

Others who attempted to cross to Sweden by rowboat included Mrs. Inge Jensen and her twin daughters, Marianne and

Birgit, who were a year and a half old at the time.[2] Both children had been injected to keep them unconscious during the
crossing, but the trip took much longer than anticipated and,
after about six hours, the effect of the sedative wore off and
Marianne began to scream. The other passengers in the boat
became frantic because they feared the noise might attract a
German patrol boat. Mrs. Jensen tried desperately, but unsuccessfully, to get her daughter to keep quiet.

Suddenly one of the men turned to her and said, "You'll have
to throw her overboard."

Mrs. Jensen clutched Marianne to her tightly.

"You have no other choice," said the man. "Otherwise we
may all be caught."

Much to Mrs. Jensen's horror, several of the other passengers
in the boat agreed with the man.

Mrs. Jensen clamped a hand over Marianne's mouth, but
Marianne struggled free and continued screaming. Finally, the
man reached over and snatched the child out of her arms. Mrs.
Jensen tried to get her back, but the other passengers grabbed
her and held her down while the man put the child's head inside
his coat and smothered her until she no longer made any sound.
He then handed the seemingly lifeless form back to Mrs.
Jensen, who didn't know whether her daughter was dead or
alive. Holding her in her arms, she rocked back and forth and
cried silently.

The other passengers, after several more hours of rowing,
with no sign of the lights of Sweden, realized that they were
lost. Totally dispirited, they stopped rowing and drifted aim-
lessly. Finally, off in the distance, they noticed the lights of a
patrol boat. They had no idea whether the boat was German
or Swedish but, feeling they had no alternative, decided to take
a chance and call out to it. Fortunately, it turned out to be
a Swedish naval vessel, which took them aboard and transported
them to the nearest Swedish port. Marianne was rushed to the
hospital, where for several weeks she hovered close to death.

She was eventually nursed back to consciousness and relative health, but still suffers today from the ordeal of having been choked into unconsciousness when she was a year and a half old back in October 1943.

That some of the refugees were willing to throw overboard or strangle into unconsciousness (and possible death) infants and children who started to cry or scream during the flight to Sweden shows to what extremes of fright and desperation they were driven during their escape.

Mendel Katlev, the leather-goods worker whose family had been hidden by a train conductor, had a crossing similar to Mrs. Jensen's, because his child's crying jeopardized the escape of the other refugees.[3]

On the night of October 4, 1943, the Katlevs, together with fifteen other Jewish refugees, were walking along the beach at Køge to the fishing boat that was to take them to Sweden. Katlev's oldest son, Harry, age seven, walked with Mrs. Katlev, while the father carried the younger boy, Mogens, age two and a half, in his arms. The night of the Katlevs' escape preceded the practice of administering injections to the children to keep them silent, and, suddenly, Mogens began to cry. Try as he would Katlev could not get him to stop.

"Strangle him," called out one of the refugees. "For God's sake strangle him or we'll all be taken by the Germans!"

Mrs. Katlev replied to the man who had made the suggestion, "I'd rather strangle you."

Mr. Katlev knew that if he could not calm Mogens, some of the other refugees might take matters into their own hands. "So," explained Mr. Katlev, "I strangled him. I didn't strangle him a lot. Just a little. Not enough to kill him, but enough to make him unconscious."

The Katlevs, together with the other refugees, were packed into the hold of the small fishing boat and they started out. The seas were rough and heavy rains poured in on them. The boat rocked and Mrs. Katlev became terribly seasick. A fellow passenger handed her a bottle of camphor and suggested that she sniff it. Misunderstanding the woman, Mrs. Katlev drank the camphor and became dizzy and ill.

As the boat entered Swedish waters, the refugees were allowed to go up on deck. Mrs. Katlev, still dizzy from the camphor, slipped and fell overboard. The boat was stopped and one of the passengers dove in after her. He succeeded in swimming back to the ship with her and her terrified husband and several of the other passengers pulled her back on deck. When her rescuer was pulled on board after her, she and her husband noticed that it was the same man who earlier had demanded that Mogens be strangled.

Difficult and unpleasant as was the Katlevs' crossing, it was not as tragic as that of their relatives the Cipikoffs, Nathan, fifty-four, his wife Helene, fifty, their sons Jacob, age twenty-three, Noah, age twenty-one, and four cousins. They were placed in a rowboat that was pulled along by a fishing boat crowded with refugees. One mile from the Swedish coast they were accidentally struck by a Swedish patrol boat, and all were drowned but Noah, who managed to swim to shore.[4]

The refugees were usually packed into the holds of the ships, but on some occasions they were hidden in huge boxes and cases which were loaded onto the ship by crane as material destined for Sweden. Carl Næsh Hendriksen, the crime reporter active in the underground, was involved in transporting the refugees to Sweden in this manner.[5] Once, after four boxes of refugees had been loaded on board a ship and a mother with her ten-month-old baby was about to enter the fifth box, the baby started to cry. Fearful that the crying would attract the attention of the Germans, Hendriksen gave the baby its first stiff drink of schnapps, which put it to sleep immediately. The mother and baby were then hoisted by crane into the hold of the ship. While the box was swinging into the hold, three German soldiers appeared with a police dog. The powder mixture of dried human blood and cocaine had been dusted on the ship, so the dog could not smell anything suspicious, but the Germans wanted to know what Hendriksen was doing with the schnapps.

"I have it because I thought you might be coming," replied Hendriksen, "and I know how you Germans appreciate some good Danish schnapps." He took them into the nearby customs shack, and, while he proceeded to get them drunk, the ship pulled away for Sweden.

In all of the crossings to Sweden, the fishermen worked closely with the inhabitants of the fishing villages up and down the coast. These local townspeople and farmers hid the Jews until the fishing boats were ready to take them across, and, on occasion, did much more than hide them. An example of the extent to which they were willing to risk their lives to help the Jews was experienced by Henry Grünbaum. In October 1943, this labor union official was hidden, together with his family and ten other refugees, in the home of a glassworker south of Copenhagen.[6] The underground had made contact with a fisherman to take the refugees to Sweden, but when the refugees showed up at the dock, the fisherman told them that he had changed his mind because he thought the voyage would be too dangerous. Their hopes unexpectedly dashed, they dragged themselves dispiritedly back to the home of the glassworker. When their host learned what had happened, he became furious and set out for the fisherman to try to convince him to change his mind. Returning half an hour later, the glassworker announced with glee that although the fisherman still would not ferry the refugees across, he would allow the glassworker to use his boat.

"Do you know how to run the boat?" asked Grünbaum.

The glassworker held up a manual of instructions which the fisherman had given him. "I can read," he said.

"You mean that you have never run a boat before?" asked Grünbaum.

"Not one that size," admitted the glassworker. "But the fisherman gave me this manual which he said would make it possible."

Grünbaum and the other refugees went into a huddle and decided not to accept the glassworker's brave but foolhardy offer. When the glassworker heard their decision, he became livid.

"What's the matter with you Jews?" he shouted. "Are you good only for being cowardly tailors and shoemakers? Don't you have any guts? If I'm willing to risk taking you, why don't you risk coming along?"

"I'll go along too," said the glassworker's wife.

"Me too," chimed in his sixteen-year-old son.

Grünbaum and the refugees were embarrassed by the reaction of the glassworker and his family.

"Let me have a look at the boat," Grünbaum asked the glassworker.

Both left the house and walked in the dark for fifteen minutes until they came to the harbor. Two Danish policemen were there. Grünbaum started to draw back.

"No, they're all right," said the glassworker.

"Are you sure?" asked Grünbaum.

"Speak to them yourself."

Grünbaum approached them. "Do you know why this boat is here?" he asked.

"Yes," replied one of the policemen. "To take the Jewish refugees to Sweden."

"And you're not going to do anything about it?"

"Why should we?"

Grünbaum looked at the boat. It was a sailboat with a motor. Perhaps the glassworker might be able to manage it.

Grünbaum returned to the house with the glassworker and announced to the refugees that he thought they should leave immediately for the boat. It was now raining very hard. The refugees, including several old people and some children, made

their way to the dock single file. Twice they had to hide in
the bushes as German soldiers passed by. They were soaked by
the rain and covered in mud. Crossing the gangplank from
the dock onto the boat, an old man fell into the water and
almost drowned. Luckily, Grünbaum's wife and some of the
other refugees managed to drag him out onto the boat.

The glassworker's wife and son accompanied them, and
for half an hour the three of them pored over the manual of
instructions without being able to start the motor. Finally,
discouraged with the motor, they managed to raise the sail
about halfway, and succeeded in putting the boat in motion.
After a few minutes, the motor mysteriously started up by itself, and the rest of the trip across the sound to Malmø was
relatively smooth and uneventful.

Naturally, not all of the crossings over the sound to Sweden
were so hazardous. But even under the best of circumstances,
the trip was seldom easy and simple. That practically all of
the Danish Jews arrived in Sweden safely is a further testament
to the skill and dedication with which the Danes carried out the
entire rescue operation.

Part Four

THE AFTERMATH

Chapter 18 THE CAPTURED

*A thousand years will pass and the guilt of Germany
will not be erased.*

—HANS FRANK, Former German Governor-General
of Occupied Poland, at the Nuremberg Trials

NOT ALL OF DENMARK'S EIGHT THOUSAND JEWS
were safely transported to Sweden. There were the unfortunate 472 who had been captured by the Germans and sent to
Theresienstadt. Among them were Ralph Oppenheim, a law
student; Benjamin Kørzen, an engineer; and Cilla Cohen, a
young bride.

Shortly after the Germans' decision to round up Denmark's
Jews, Ralph Oppenheim, together with his sister and parents,
went into hiding in the summer house of a friend at Rungsted,
a small town on the seacoast between Copenhagen and Elsinore.[1] There they made contact with a fisherman who agreed
to row the Oppenheims the two and a half miles across the
sound to Sweden. The trip was to take three to four hours,
but because of fog and a heavy storm it took considerably
longer. In addition, after several hours the boat sprang a leak.
The fisherman and the Oppenheims took off their shoes to bail
out the water, but the boat began filling up faster than they

could bail. The situation seemed hopeless until a large Danish fishing boat came into view, pulled alongside and took them aboard. From the boat's captain they learned that they were only twenty minutes off the Swedish coast. Mr. Oppenheim told the captain that he and his family were Jewish refugees, and pleaded with him to take them to Sweden. The captain refused on the grounds that to do so would be breaking the law. He agreed, however, to take them to Aarhus, in Jutland, which was his destination. Several hours later, when the boat pulled into Aarhus, Gestapo officers were on the dock waiting for the Oppenheims. The fishing boat captain, a Danish Nazi, had wired ahead. Seeing the Gestapo officers, Mr. Oppenheim distributed to his wife and children small bottles of poison he had earlier received from his family physician, and the entire family attempted to commit suicide by swallowing the contents of the bottles. The Germans noticed what was going on, and, as soon as the boat docked, rushed the Oppenheims to the local hospital, where their stomachs were pumped out. Ralph Oppenheim regained consciousness four days later. He learned that his sister and parents, who had also been saved, had regained consciousness a day earlier. From the Aarhus hospital, the Oppenheims were transferred to Horserød Concentration Camp in Denmark, where Ralph was told by the commandant: "The arrest of you Jews has caused quite a commotion in Copenhagen. The students have gone out on strike, the University has closed down all week and protests are pouring in from the church and businessmen's organizations. I know of no other country where this has happened. I myself don't approve of the way the Jews are being persecuted. I'm a reasonable man. But at the same time I am an officer in the Wehrmacht and I have to obey orders. I'm sure you understand."

After two weeks in Horserød, the Oppenheims, together with the hundreds of other Danish Jews captured by the Germans, were taken by boat to the town of Warnemünde in Germany, where they were transferred to the cattle cars that

were to take them to Theresienstadt. While being piled into
the cattle cars, they were surrounded by hundreds of local
German townspeople of all ages. Ralph was shocked to find
that the German civilians expressed no disapproval of the
brutality with which the guards whipped into the cattle cars
those who moved slowly, such as the old people, cripples and
children. On the contrary, the Germans spat upon the Jews
and called them "scum of the earth," "Jewish swine," and far
more obscene names. Ralph never realized until that moment
how endemic anti-Semitism was to the German people as a
whole. The doors of the cattle cars were sealed shut and Ralph
was unable to tell the exact number of days it took to get to
Theresienstadt, but he guessed that it was between two and
four days. During that time the cattle-car doors were never
opened, and there was nothing to eat, nothing to drink and no
place to urinate or empty one's bowels. The stench was un-
bearable, and there was a severe lack of oxygen. By the time
Theresienstadt was reached, there were fifteen corpses in
Ralph's cattle car. His own family survived.

Like the Oppenheims, Benjamin Kørzen and his wife were
captured because of a pro-Nazi Danish informer.[2] The Elsinore
Sewing Club had made arrangements for the Kørzens to board
a fishing boat at Gilleleje. When they arrived, they were told
that the Gestapo was in the harbor and it would be necessary
for them to go into hiding for a while. They were led to Gilleleje Church and hidden in the attic. Other refugees who were
supposed to leave that evening from Gilleleje were also taken
to the church, and by 6 P.M. there were sixty-two refugees in
the attic. The underground agent told the refugees that they
had nothing to worry about, that something was being done to
get the Gestapo out of the harbor and permit the refugees to get
to their ships. When the refugees asked for details, they were
told that a false air-raid alarm would be set off which would
get the Gestapo men to leave their posts and make the road

clear for the refugees. This explanation calmed their fears and
they stretched out on the floor of the attic to await the alarm.
They never heard it, because before it could be set off an informer who had noticed the large influx of refugees into Gilleleje Church telephoned Gestapo Chief Juhl in Elsinore.

While waiting with the others for the false air-raid alarm,
Kørzen found a place near the attic window, and every once in
a while he would look out. After several hours, he saw a sight
that made him hold his breath—groups of German soldiers were
setting up machine guns on the church lawn. Not wishing to
panic the others, he kept silent and watched in horror as several
truckloads of heavily armed German troops arrived and surrounded the church. Finally, there was the pounding down-
stairs on the church door. The refugees became frightened and
wondered aloud who could be knocking. If it was the underground, reasoned one of the refugees, surely they would have
the keys to open the locked doors. Kørzen could not immediately bring himself to announce what he had seen. It wasn't
until one of the soldiers outside shouted, "If you don't open
the door, we'll shoot it open!" that Kørzen was able to say,
"It's no use. It's the Germans. We might as well open the door.
We'll have to give ourselves up."

A young boy seated next to Kørzen jumped to his feet.
"Not me," he said. With the agility of a monkey he climbed to
the bell tower above the attic and hid among the bells. He was
the only one who managed to escape. All of the others were
captured and sent to Theresienstadt.

Unlike the Oppenheims and Kørzens, Cilla Cohen and her
family were not captured through an informer, but because of
stupidity on the part of an underground agent.[3] After hearing
about the German roundup, Mrs. Cohen and her husband, a
butcher, together with Mrs. Cohen's parents, went into hiding
at a friend's summer house in Hundige. On October 5, a young
underground agent arrived to take them by car to the seacoast

town of Kastrup, about twenty minutes south of Copenhagen, where, he informed them, a boat would be waiting to take them to Sweden. They arrived at Kastrup at 11 A.M. and parked a block away from the dock. Through the windshield, Mrs. Cohen could see refugees boarding a boat tied up at the dock.

"Is that the boat we're supposed to get on?" she asked.

"Yes," replied the underground agent.

"Well, why don't we get on it?"

"Not yet," said the agent. "There's one other person we must wait for here before boarding the boat, a young girl, a Communist, who is wanted by the Germans."

Ten minutes passed without any sign of the girl. Mrs. Cohen and her relatives became anxious.

"What time was the girl supposed to be here?" she asked.

"She is late," replied the underground agent. "She was supposed to be here waiting for us when we arrived, at eleven o'clock."

"Couldn't we get on the boat meanwhile?"

"No. I'm supposed to deliver the five of you together. We must wait for her. I had better move the car to avoid suspicion."

For the next forty minutes they kept circling the block, looking in vain for the Communist girl. The Cohens became increasingly nervous. Mrs. Cohen felt that the constant circling of the block was causing suspicion rather than avoiding it. For about the first twenty minutes, each time the car circled the block and came within sight of the boat, Mrs. Cohen could see one or two additional refugees sneaking on board. Later, no one seemed to board the boat.

"No one else seems to be getting on board," pointed out Mrs. Cohen. "Perhaps the boat is ready to leave. Perhaps we'll miss it."

"Don't worry," said the underground agent, "the boat won't leave without us."

One thing that particularly worried Mrs. Cohen was her father's long beard. It made him readily identifiable as a Jew.

She knew that if the automobile were stopped by the Germans, there would be trouble. She and her husband did their utmost to persuade the young underground agent to let them board the boat.

"All right," said the agent, finally, "we'll wait here five more minutes and if that stupid girl doesn't come by then, all of you can leave the car for the boat."

They remained parked a block away from the dock. Before the five minutes were up, a German soldier opened the door of the car and, at gunpoint, ordered them to step outside. "You're Jews, aren't you?" he asked.

They did not reply.

"And you're here to try to get to Sweden?"

"What do you want from us?" pleaded Mr. Cohen. "What have we ever done to you? Why don't you let us go?"

"Put your hands up in the air!" barked the soldier.

While the others did as they were told, Mr. Cohen put his hand in his pocket and took out his wallet. "I'll give you all the money we have," he said, "only please let us go."

The soldier looked at the money and, for a moment, seemed to debate with himself whether to take it. His decision was made for him a moment later when a German officer joined him.

"Jews trying to escape?" asked the officer.

"*Jawohl*," replied the soldier.

Mr. Cohen held his wallet out to the officer. "Take the money," he begged, "both of you. You can divide it between you."

"Put that away," snapped the officer. "Bribery is a crime for those who make the offer as well as for those who accept it."

"Can't you let us go?" asked Mr. Cohen.

"Of course I can't let you go. But your fears are ridiculous," said the officer. "You have nothing to worry about. Do you think we're beasts? Do you think we're inhuman? Do I look like a torturer or a murderer? You must forget all the propaganda, all the rumors and lies you have heard about us. Do you know what is going to happen to you? You're going to be taken to a work camp in Germany where your efforts will be guided into productive labor. That is all that is going to happen to you."

They were taken to Vestre Prison, where for several days Mrs. Cohen was separated from her husband and parents. She rejoined them again in Horserød Concentration Camp in Denmark. Finally, together with the Oppenheims and Kørzens, the Cohens were shipped to Theresienstadt.

Theresienstadt was considered a model camp—in fact, the best of the concentration camps—and to it were sent not only the captured Danish Jews, but those whom the Germans considered the elite of Jewish prisoners from all of their occupied countries and from Germany itself. From Germany came those Jews who had been honored under the Kaiser and the Weimar Republic for their achievements in science and for their heroism in World War I. Many of the German Jews at Theresienstadt had lost limbs fighting for the fatherland during World War I and had been decorated with the Iron Cross. For about 10,000 of those who entered Theresienstadt, including all of the Danish Jews, it was to be their one and only concentration camp. For about 300,000 others, less lucky, it was to be only a stopover on their way to the death camps of Auschwitz, Neuengamme, Bergen-Belsen, Buchenwald and Dachau.

Although considered a "model" camp, Theresienstadt had four crematoria working day and night and its *Kleine Festung*, or small fortress, where S.S. guards were given a free hand, and where torture and murder were the order of the day.

Immediately upon arrival at Theresienstadt, the Oppenheims, Kørzens and Cohens, together with their fellow Danish prisoners, were given cigarettes and were greeted by Professor Paul Epstein, a German-Jewish sociologist, who introduced himself to them as the "Mayor" of the camp.[4] They were then led into

the camp mess hall, where they ate a hearty meal on clean
white tablecloths. Along with their desserts they were handed
sheets of paper and stamped envelopes and told to write home
to their friends in Denmark about conditions in the camp. After
their letters were completed and taken away from them, they
were brought face to face with the reality of what life was
to be for them at Theresienstadt. Those were the last tablecloths they were to see, and that was the last decent meal they
were to have, for a long, long time. Their average day's meals
were to consist of ersatz coffee for breakfast, potato soup occasionally containing a sliver of unrecognizable meat for lunch
and potato soup or ersatz coffee for dinner.[5]

Several days after their arrival they were shown what would
happen to them if they dared to protest against their meager
rations: fifteen young Jewish boys and girls from Czechoslovakia who had protested were publicly hanged in the center of
the camp.

In addition to the hanging of the young Czechs, the Danes
witnessed several other events shortly after their arrival at
Theresienstadt which served as examples of what life was to be
like at this "model" camp. To make room for the 472 new
Danish arrivals, a number of barracks were emptied of Polish
Jewish children by shipping them to Auschwitz to be extermi-
nated.[6] On Armistice Day, November 11, 1943, as retribution
for the shame Germany was forced to suffer in her defeat of
World War I, all of the prisoners of Theresienstadt were made
to stand in an open field for twenty hours. During this ordeal,
many collapsed, and several of the older people died.[7] Then
there was the organization at the camp by the S.S. of an old
men's "free-for-all." About a hundred of the camp's oldest
prisoners were gathered together in an open field. Many of
them were so ill and feeble that they could remain upright only
by supporting each other by standing back to back. The S.S.
officers ordered the old men to start beating one another. When
they refused at first, the officers went among them and began

pummeling them with their fists as hard as they could. Fearful of being crippled, the old men began to strike out at each other. The S.S. shouted that they wanted the men to hit as hard as they could, and they set an example by striking some of the old men until they became unconscious. A desperate mass insanity seized the old men, and they "put all their strength into the blows they gave each other."[8]

If, after these events, the Danes needed any further indication of the type of treatment they were to receive at the hands of their German captors, they had finally the example of what happened to the Dutch-Jewish artist caught making pencil sketches of life in Theresienstadt: a German doctor cut off all his fingers.[9]

All of the Danish prisoners were given work to do at Theresienstadt. Ralph Oppenheim's job was to carry corpses to the crematoria and, after they were burned, to throw their ashes into the river Eger. The Kørzens were given manual labor. Cilla Cohen was made a doctor's assistant, and her husband was made to work a pneumatic drill on a rock pile.

During the first weeks at Theresienstadt, the Danish prisoners lost a tremendous amount of weight and over thirty of them died. Cilla Cohen lost over twenty pounds during her first ten days at the camp, and, after collapsing on the job, was admitted as a patient to the hospital where she worked, suffering from malnutrition. In the ward to which she was assigned, she was stripped of her clothes for a medical examination. When her fellow patients saw her naked, those who could walk came over to her and began touching her. At first she became frightened, but then she realized that they were fascinated by her suntan. She had spent the summer on the beach at Rungsted, and still had a rather dark tan. "They wanted to feel for themselves this miracle, suntanned skin," Mrs. Cohen later wrote. "It was not me they wanted to touch. It was the sun, it was freedom, it was a paradise lost."[10]

Things went from bad to worse for the Danes during their

first months at Theresienstadt. Arthur Friediger, a young chemist, described the effect on his fellow Danes: "Occasionally the horrible conditions made people act in an extremely noble manner, almost like saints. They would not think of themselves. They would think only of trying to help others more hungry than themselves, in greater pain or difficulty than themselves. But most often conditions in the camp brought out the worst in people. People you knew from Copenhagen as decent, interesting human beings who would never hurt a fly suddenly took to stealing, to lying, even to denouncing, just to get a little more bread. When they denounced others, that was the most awful thing of all, for it meant that those denounced would be sent on the next transport to one of the death camps."[11]

Friediger's job at Theresienstadt was the laying of water pipes in the town outside the camp. Together with some of the other workers, he would smuggle outside the camp the clothes of prisoners who had died or had been shipped to the death camps and exchange these garments with the local Czechs for food and cigarettes. For several weeks Friediger laid water pipes near the railroad station of Bohuschowitz, and during this time he would see trainload after trainload of Jews in open railroad cars traveling on their way to the death camps. Seeing these people was his most horrible experience at Theresienstadt. The Jews, including many children, were all emaciated, half-dead, some already corpses and skeletons. Hundreds of German soldiers, German civilian workers and local Czech townspeople witnessed these open trainloads. They voiced no protest. Occasionally, a sympathetic Czech farmer would give to Friediger and his fellow prisoners tomatoes to take back to the other inmates of the camp.

One of the worst things about life in Theresienstadt was the uncertainty of not knowing how long one was going to remain there. Several times a week trainloads of prisoners left for Auschwitz or Neuengamme or Bergen-Belsen or Dachau. The Danes never knew when it would be their turn.

But the Danish Jews never left Theresienstadt Concentration Camp. And what is even more astounding, of the 472 Danish prisoners at the camp, only fifty-three died there, and these were mainly old people who succumbed en route or during the first weeks due to malnutrition. After January 1944, while thousands of other prisoners died of starvation, not a single Dane died for lack of food. While all around them prisoners were dying of illness and disease, the Danes remained in relatively good health. There is no mystery about this. The explanation, the plain truth of the matter, is that the Danish government and people were relentless in their concern for their Jewish nationals in Theresienstadt, while the governments and peoples of the other countries were largely apathetic about their Jewish nationals in concentration camps.

At the Bermuda Refugee Conference, held in the spring of 1943, representatives of the World Jewish Congress asked the delegates to enter into negotiations with the Axis countries to promote the distribution of food parcels to ghettoes and concentration camps where the Jews were being starved to death. The delegates rejected consideration of these proposals on the grounds that it would be unfair to put Jews on a priority list for relief.[12] According to British historian Malcolm Hay, "The only result of the Bermuda Refugee Conference was to strengthen Hitler's conviction that the world did not really care very much what happened to the Jews, and to fortify his resolution to exterminate them."[13]

As a rule, the world did *not* care. But Denmark *did*. The Danish government was constantly concerned about the welfare of the Jews who had been captured, and it took steps to aid them. One of its first measures was to enter the homes of those arrested, to assemble clothes which it thought might be needed and to send these clothes to Theresienstadt. In addition, the King and other members of the Danish government maintained a steady barrage of inquiries to the Germans to determine whether the Jewish prisoners were being properly treated. More important, the Danish government, working with a number of private individuals, organized a regular delivery of food parcels to every one of the Danish Jews in Theresienstadt. These parcels served a double purpose. Containing food and drugs, they were, more than anything else, responsible for the physical well-being of the prisoners. They also served as an effective stimulant, showing the prisoners that they were not forgotten, that their government and fellow countrymen cared about them. Several former employees of the Copenhagen office of American Express—Kaj Christiansen, Ole Evensen, G. Thorbjørnsen and A. R. Frederiksen—organized thirty-five people to work full time sending these packages to Theresienstadt. Christiansen and several of the others had printed and attached to the parcels a two-way mailing piece which demanded the signature of the receiver and had to be sent back to the sender. Most of the other types of relief parcels sent during World War II had no such forms and so the parcels were stolen by the Germans. But when the Germans, with their typical bureaucratic efficiency, saw that signed receipts had to be sent back to the senders, they passed all of the Danish parcels on to the proper addressees. Technically, food parcels could be received only if sent by relatives, and so the senders pretended to be Christian relatives of the prisoners, sending along with the parcels letters addressed to "Dear Uncle ———" or "Dear Aunt ———." The food parcels made the Danish prisoners the most important prisoners at Theresienstadt. They were sought after, befriended and envied. According to Cilla Cohen, Danish girls, regardless of their looks, were treated by the handsomest male prisoners as though they were movie queens, while girl prisoners of other nationalities "clung to Danish boys as they would have to handsome men in uniform in peacetime."[14] Food was of such importance in Theresienstadt that all social status revolved around it. Anyone who had any connection with food was considered to be of the highest social standing. A former professor, doctor, aristocrat or high government official was looked upon simply as the lavatory attendant or ditchdigger he was at the camp. On the other hand, a cook, baker, or dishwasher—anyone with a direct or indirect connection with food—was a member of the elite, for he was a possible source of an extra sliver of meat, an egg, a slice of bread, a cup of soup.

In addition to arranging for the sending of food and medical supplies to the inmates of Theresienstadt, the Danish government was tireless in its requests to the German authorities for permission for a Danish Red Cross commission to inspect conditions at the camp. Finally, in February 1944, the Germans agreed to allow Danish authorities to visit the camp in the late spring. In order to make a favorable impression on the Danish Commission, Theresienstadt was completely redecorated. New barracks were constructed, old buildings were repainted and new beds, furniture and clothing were given to the prisoners. Those prisoners who bore signs of torture or had been crippled were shipped out of the camp. The streets running through Theresienstadt were cleaned with a thoroughness and care usually reserved for parquet floors. Concerts, lectures and sporting events were organized at the camp, and a special children's pavilion was built and stocked with equipment for a wide variety of children's activities. A sham self-government council was created, with Professor Paul Epstein as its head. Epstein was given his own apartment on the camp grounds, was dressed in tails, pin-striped trousers and a top hat and was given a limousine with an S.S. officer posing as a chauffeur to drive him around. Worthless Theresienstadt marks were even printed to show that the prisoners were paid for their labor.[15]

The Danish Commission, headed by Dr. Frantz Hvass of the Danish Foreign Ministry and Dr. Juel Henningsen of the Department of Health, arrived at Theresienstadt on June 23. Several days before their arrival, the prisoners had been warned that any complaints to the visiting Danes would result in the severest consequences. For the Commission's benefit, table-

cloths, new dinnerware and flowers were put on all the tables
in the mess hall, and the waiters, wearing not only clean uniforms but spotless white gloves, served a banquet.

Addressing the prisoners, Dr. Hvass said: "The King sends
his best regards to you, and I also have best greetings from
Bishop Fuglsang-Damgaard, who asked me to tell you that he
prays for you. . . ."[16]

Rabbi Friediger, Arthur Friediger's father, later wrote: "It
is impossible for me to describe the feeling which penetrated
my heart in that moment. If one understands what is meant by
the word 'revelation'—then one can realize what I felt when
these words were said to me. *The King sends his best regards
. . .*! Was it not a blessed country where a king and a bishop
send regards to a Jew?"

As Dr. Hvass and Dr. Henningsen passed among the Danish
Jews to shake their hands, a fellow prisoner remarked to Rabbi
Friediger: "It is now that I feel redeemed as a human being in
my own eyes. Once again I have a certain value as a man. These
Danes have given it back to me."

Professor Epstein acted as the official guide for Hvass and
Henningsen, taking them to various points in the camp in his
limousine. Each time the formally attired "mayor" and his
guests entered or left the car, they were saluted smartly by Epstein's "chauffeur." Following to the letter his instructions from
the Germans, Epstein kept up a constant chatter on how wonderful things were at the camp.

That the visitors to Theresienstadt were impressed can be
seen in a glowing report they delivered a month later to the
International Red Cross in Stockholm. They described
Theresienstadt more as an ideal suburban community than a
concentration camp. After the war, Dr. Hvass claimed that he
had purposely reported conditions more favorable than he had
found them in order to encourage the Germans to allow the
Danes to continue shipments of foodstuffs and medical supplies
to the camp. He also claimed that he and Henningsen knew

that the Germans had improved conditions at the camp for their inspection, but that he did not want to say anything that might antagonize the Germans into forbidding the food shipments.[17]

The Theresienstadt prisoners benefited from the visit of the Danish Commission, because although food rations were reduced to normal immediately after the departure of Hvass and Henningsen, all of the physical improvements of the camp remained.

Professor Epstein was repaid by the Germans in an ironic way for being their lackey and willing tool. For two days following the departure from the camp of the Danish Commission, the Gestapo officer who had been posing as Epstein's chauffeur continued to drive him around the camp in the limousine, snapping to attention every time he opened the door for him, and always calling him "Herr Mayor." On the third day, Epstein was informed that he was to receive a special acknowledgment for his good behavior before the Danish Red Cross Commission. His "chauffeur" drove him to a deserted part of the camp and put a bullet through his head.

Chapter 19 SABOTAGE!

Every time the factory is bombed and burned,
The heat lightning of liberty is set on fire.

—KARL ROOS

BEFORE OCTOBER 1943, Danish resistance activities were few in number. After that date they increased tremendously. Until then, only a handful of saboteurs carried out significant resistance operations. After it, the membership of the organized Danish resistance increased almost overnight to forty thousand.

The most important single factor responsible for the sudden explosive growth of the Danish resistance movement was the German persecution of the Danish Jews. The largest number of sabotage acts carried out in any one month of the occupation occurred in November 1943, a month after the attempted roundup. In December, the Gestapo chief of Denmark wrote in his report to Berlin that this was a direct consequence of the effort to arrest the Danish Jews. Ole Lippman, one of the leaders of the resistance, stated: "The Danes, being a peace-loving and easygoing people, had been reluctant for several years to take an active part in the resistance movement. But when the Germans started to persecute the Jews, when people had to hide relatives and friends, it meant that they were taking the first step in engaging in illegal activities against the Germans. This encouraged them to go even further and, as a consequence, the resistance movement grew enormously."[1]

According to Danish historian Ole Barfoed, "it was the greatest fault and stupidity of the Germans to start Jewish pogroms in Denmark. But in a way, one could also say that it was also a very good thing—actually a 'service' that the Germans performed. What happened to the Jews strongly accentuated the resistance and united people—not politically, but on a human plane. The net of contacts that the saving of the Jews created throughout Denmark showed itself to be most useful for the later development of the resistance movement. New channels were developed . . . without the aid of which the underground movement would have looked very different."[2] The new channels mentioned by Barfoed refer to the escape routes across the sound first developed to transport the Jews and later used for saboteurs and arms.

Christian Kisling, the sea captain who had gone to work as a driver for a salvage company rather than sail for the Nazis, was one of many who became saboteurs as a direct consequence of becoming involved in the rescue of the Jews. "At first public opinion was against sabotage," said Captain Kisling. "But then, once the Germans started in with the Jews and we had to help them to escape, we got a taste of what it was like to fight the Germans, and we liked it. We thought, now that the Jews are safe in Sweden—let's continue, let's go all the way."

Captain Kisling's specialty was the planting of fire bombs. Because of his job with the salvage company, he was in an ideal position to insure the effectiveness of his operations. "Sometimes I would be called in to drive an ambulance or a fire engine to the aid of a factory or German fortification that I had helped blow up," explained Kisling. "It was wonderful to be able to come back and see at close range how well the job had been done. Sometimes, when a job hadn't gone too well, by being on the spot as a rescuer, I was able to remedy matters by placing another charge."[3]

Jørgen Knudsen, the ambulance driver, was like Christian Kisling, another example of a Dane who became involved in sabotage activities after helping the Jews to escape to Sweden. Although he worked full time for the underground, he continued to receive his regular monthly wages from Bispebjerg Hospital—thanks to an arrangement made by Dr. Køster. In addition to transporting by ambulance saboteurs and Allied airmen who had been shot down over Denmark, Knudsen smuggled weapons, distributed illegal newspapers and delivered illegal mail. Another of his assignments was to pick up arms "drops" parachuted to the Danish underground from British planes. One night the entire drop consisted of whiskey and cigarettes. A note explained that it was in appreciation of the work Knudsen and his associates had done in smuggling British airmen out of Denmark.

In the winter of 1944, Knudsen was sent to warn a policeman working in the underground that his activities had been discovered by the Gestapo. Borrowing a physician's automobile, he drove to the policeman's address as quickly as possible. He arrived too late. When he rang the bell, the door was opened by a Gestapo officer. In the background, Knudsen could see three other Gestapo officers and a German soldier.

"What are you doing here?" asked the Gestapo officer.

"I'm here to visit my friend," said Knudsen matter-of-factly.

He was yanked into the room and shoved onto a couch. "What connection do you have with this man?"

"We're friends," replied Knudsen. "We were in the Army together. What's going on here? Has something happened to him?"

"How did you get here?"

"I walked."

The Gestapo officer gave a whispered instruction to a German soldier. The soldier left the apartment.

"May I go to the bathroom?" asked Knudsen.

Permission was granted. Knudsen flushed the car key down the toilet. When he returned to the living room, the German soldier asked him whether the physician's automobile parked outside the building belonged to him.

"No," replied Knudsen.

He was thoroughly searched for the car key.

"Now are you satisfied?" asked Knudsen.

The Gestapo officers were not satisfied. They kept Knudsen in the apartment for several hours, and, while questioning him about his connections with the policeman he had come to visit, kept drinking from several bottles of schnapps which they had found in the apartment. When there was nothing more to drink, they told Knudsen that they were taking him to Gestapo Headquarters. The four Gestapo officers took Knudsen into their car. They were now quite drunk.

"I don't think," said one of the Gestapo officers, "that we can show up at Gestapo Headquarters in the condition we're in. The others might get jealous."

The three other officers laughed. "Let's go to a bar and really get drunk," suggested one of them.

The leader of the group turned to Knudsen. "If we let you go now, will you promise to be at Gestapo Headquarters at ten o'clock tomorrow morning?"

"Of course," said Knudsen.

The following morning, Knudsen showed up at Gestapo Headquarters. He had decided that this would be the safest thing to do; it would show his belief in his innocence. He also knew that the Germans had no evidence that he was involved in underground activities, aside from his having appeared at his friend's apartment. The Gestapo men seemed pleased that Knudsen had appeared, and although their questioning was long, it was proper and even friendly. After several hours, one of the Gestapo officers asked in a gentle, almost kind way, "Are you sure that there is nothing—really nothing that you have done against us? Come, I give you my word that we are going to let you go free. We really have nothing to hold you on. But, just for the fun of it, off the record, isn't there anything that you have done against us?"

Knudsen was so taken in by the officer's apparent charm that he admitted that he had helped Jews to escape to Sweden.

"But why?"

"Because I felt it had to be done. I just couldn't stand by and do nothing while friends of mine were being persecuted."

"So you have Jewish friends?"

"Yes."

"And you did not like the way we were treating them?"

"No."

The gentle Gestapo officer signaled two guards, and while they held Knudsen, the officer repeatedly punched him in the face until he became unconscious. He came to several hours later, when, true to the officer's promise, he was released from the prison. The beating he had received encouraged Knudsen to work harder than ever in the resistance movement.

At the end of January 1945, Knudsen received an assignment to smuggle sixteen badly wounded saboteurs from Denmark to Sweden. They were put on a tugboat which, because of the coal shortage, used hay as a fuel. Naturally, the boat had to hold huge amounts of this odd and inefficient fuel, and under the stacks of hay were hidden the saboteurs. Because of bad weather, bad communications and, finally, a sudden emergency tugging operation to which the boat was assigned, it took three days to get to Sweden. The saboteurs had to remain hidden all this time under the hay. Fortunately, there was enough food aboard the boat to feed them, but Knudsen had to inject them constantly with morphine to keep them quiet. One of the sixteen died. When the boat arrived in Halmstad, Sweden, a Swedish policeman, who by now had gotten used to the regular arrival of Danish refugees and saboteurs, cheerfully called out for the Danes to hop out onto the deck. When Knudsen and the Danish sailors aboard the boat started lifting out the one dead and fifteen badly wounded saboteurs, the Swedish policeman suddenly changed the cheerful expression on his face. He immediately put in a call for all available ambulances in Halmstad to come to the docks. He then told Knudsen that for the very first time he now saw the seriousness of the situation in Denmark. Knudsen remained in Sweden with the wounded men for the next five months, until the end of the war.[4]

In the explosive growth of the Danish resistance, the worst fears of Renthe-Fink, Hannecken and Mildner were realized. They were finally turning upon the Germans with such fury that Field Marshal Viscount Montgomery was later to describe the Danish resistance as "second to none." In no other occupied country was sabotage used with such deadly effectiveness as in Denmark. By the war's end, there had been 2,548 acts of sabotage committed against factories, German military installations and ports, and 2,156 acts of sabotage committed against railroad installations. The railroad sabotage was so disruptive that in 1944 the train run across Jutland, Germany's main line of communication with her military forces in Norway, which normally took five hours, took ten days. During the Battle of the Bulge, when the Germans called for a full division stationed in Norway to join the fighting at Ardennes, the troops reached their destination a week too late, as a result of the Danish sabotage of the rail system.[5]

The saboteurs acted not only against German forces, but against Danes cooperating with Germans in business or as informers. During the occupation the resistance movement was forced to liquidate informers as a matter of self-defense. In all, 170 executions of Danish collaborators and informers were carried out.[6]

The saboteurs were not without the traditional Danish sense of humor. When Crown Princess Ingrid gave birth to a daughter, the Danish underground, in lieu of the Danish armed forces' traditional twenty-one-gun salute, set off twenty-one acts of sabotage. Mogens Fisker, a Danish film distributor, supplied the saboteurs with a number of anti-German films he had smuggled into the country via the Allied legations in Sweden. The members of the underground were thus able to enjoy such banned films as *The Moon Is Down, In Which We Serve, Desert Victory, The Fight for Stalingrad, Donald Duck in Germany* and *Lambeth Walk*. In addition, the saboteurs would raid movie houses where German films were being shown and force the projectionists at gunpoint to substitute anti-German propaganda films. After the Allied invasion of Normandy, the saboteurs distributed signs throughout Copenhagen reading: "Learn English before the English come." After they were torn down by the Germans, new signs appeared: "Learn German before the Germans go."

After the exodus of the Jews, Mogens Staffeldt turned his bookshop into an assignment center for Danish saboteurs parachuted back into their country after receiving training in England. It was in the back of Staffeldt's store—the same place from which hundreds of Jews had left for Sweden- that the saboteurs set out to blow up factories, disrupt rail communications and liquidate traitors and informers.

On February 16, 1944, twelve saboteurs left Staffeldt's store to carry out a complicated sabotage action in the southern part of the country near the German border. The following day three Gestapo officers entered the bookstore and arrested Staffeldt. He was taken to Gestapo Headquarters, where he was told that all twelve saboteurs had been captured and that one of the twelve had implicated Staffeldt. The Gestapo wanted the names of all of Staffeldt's underground contacts. The bookshop-owner denied engaging in any illegal activities other than helping Jews to escape. After several hours of questioning, during which Staffeldt steadfastly stuck to his story, the Gestapo ordered that the bookstore be raided and searched for arms. Staffeldt was most surprised to learn from the Gestapo a few hours later that no arms had been found there. Christian Kisling, upon learning of Staffeldt's arrest, had daringly entered the store and removed all arms.

From Gestapo Headquarters, Staffeldt was transferred to Vestre Prison, where he underwent several weeks of intense questioning. Although he was uncooperative, he was not tortured. Several times, however, his interviewers lost patience and struck him.

Less fortunate than Staffeldt was a fellow prisoner and close friend, Svend Otto Nielsen, a mathematics teacher turned saboteur. Nielsen, in attempting to escape from the Germans, had been shot eight times and his thighbone was broken. To get him to talk, the Germans not only questioned him daily, but tortured him by repeatedly allowing his broken thighbone to heal and then breaking it again and rubbing the fractured ends against each other. In addition, the Germans allowed him no medical attention. He was never carried to the bathroom or permitted to wash. His mattress was a cake of blood, feces and pus. Finally, after four and a half months of torture, the Germans sat him up in a chair, carried him into the courtyard and shot him. He was permitted to write two letters the night before he was shot. To his brother he wrote: ". . . up until now I have taken it all strangely, calmly, almost with a smile. If God wills it, I will meet my death in the same manner. I want to die with dignity. Now it is all over. I wonder if one hears the bang of the guns or if one is dead before. Well, I will soon know. I am not scared to die and I hope I will not become so—but one should not show off too early. There are limits for courage." And to his wife and daughter he wrote: "Do not grieve for me, I do not wish it. Be sensible. You cannot change anything of what has happened. Myself, I am cool and calm. I took my verdict without complaint and nervousness, with a little smile. Yes, you can become like that. These five months have hardened me. It is now five in the morning. I have just been given some wonderful sandwiches and am enjoying my coffee with a good cigar from 'old times.' I hope that the

Almighty will let me meet my death as calmly as He gave me strength to carry these months of pain. I wish for peace soon to come in the world, peace in your minds, peace and happiness for our little country. And in my last prayer I will pray for your future. Loving regards and thoughts. Svend."[7]

Knowing the condition of his friend Nielsen, hearing his screams as he was tortured and finally learning of his execution in no way weakened Staffeldt's resolve to refuse to tell the Germans anything that might harm the underground. Seeing that they were getting nowhere with him, the Germans sent Staffeldt to Horserød Concentration Camp. There he was sentenced to death, but before the sentence was carried out he managed to escape and make his way back to Copenhagen. From October 1, 1944, to November 15, 1944, Staffeldt remained in hiding in the homes of friends. He learned that his wife had made her way to Sweden. He also learned that his younger brother Jørgen had been picked up by the Germans and sent to Neuengamme, where he was later killed. On November 15, Staffeldt, together with fourteen other saboteurs, boarded an old fishing boat in Nyhavn. The saboteurs were stretched out on the floor of the hold of the ship and covered with cases of herring. Over the herring, surrounding metal tubes through which they breathed, were placed three feet of ice. The herring acted as a buffer between the saboteurs and the ice. While the last of the ice was being put in the hold, several suspicious German soldiers arrived. The fishermen were ordered to remove the ice. When the soldiers saw the fish underneath, they decided to look no further. The ice was replaced and the boat was permitted to leave the dock. Three hours later the boat was met in Swedish waters by a Swedish naval vessel which took Staffeldt and his companions to Sweden.[8]

Staffeldt's friend Jens Lillelund fared much better than Staffeldt. Despite the fact that he was one of the most active and effective of all the saboteurs—responsible for blowing up the largest exhibition hall in Scandinavia (it was to have been turned into a German Army barracks) as well as many arms factories and railroad installations—he was never caught by the Germans. In 1950, when Winston Churchill visited Denmark, Lillelund was presented to him as one of Denmark's heroes. As they shook hands, Churchill said, "Yes, Lillelund, I've heard a great deal about you." Lillelund replied, "Thank you, Mr. Churchill, I've heard a great deal about you." The Prime Minister broke into hearty laughter.[9]

In Aarhus, one of the important saboteurs was Mrs. Ina Haxen. After working with Professor Richard Ege in the rescue of the Jews, she had returned to her family in November 1943. She found herself bored in the role of an Aarhus matron, and wanted very much to be part of what was now a growing Danish resistance movement. Her opportunity came a month later when a bearded gentleman calling himself "Mr. Rasmussen" and posing as an engineer showed up in Aarhus. Mr. Haxen discovered that he was in reality the Danish writer Peter P. Rohde, who had just escaped from two years of imprisonment in a German concentration camp. Mrs. Haxen persuaded her husband to let "Mr. Rasmussen" stay at their home, where, during the following year, she helped him edit the nationally distributed resistance newspaper, *Free Denmark*. In addition, she acted as a courier and arms-carrier in local sabotage actions. In December of 1944, Rohde was captured by the Gestapo. He was tortured until he became deaf. Mrs. Haxen escaped to Sweden. She resolved that after she had learned to shoot a gun she would return to Denmark to kill the man who had tortured Rohde.[10]

The accomplishments of Danish sabotage against the Germans were spectacular. Through underground contact with the English, saboteurs were able to direct R.A.F. bombers to destroy completely Gestapo Headquarters in Copenhagen and Aarhus. In the disruption of German rail communications with

Norway, in the blowing up of the huge Dansk Riffelsyndikat and Globus arms factories and in the destruction of German V-2 component factories located in Denmark, the sabotage actions had a significance beyond national boundaries.

One of the most important of the sabotage actions was the general strike throughout Denmark from June 26 to July 3. It is particularly fascinating because it erupted, like the rescue of the Jews, as a spontaneous mass action.

In June 1944, as reprisal for the increasing sabotage actions, the Germans began murdering Danish patriots. Included among them was Kaj Munk, the well-known Danish poet and playwright, who was found in the woods with five bullets through his face. In addition, the Germans instituted what they called "clearing murders." Each time a German soldier was shot or an informer liquidated, the Germans let loose on the streets of Copenhagen the Schalburg Corps. In addition to destroying theaters, homes and amusement parks, including the beloved Tivoli, these Danish Nazis would open fire at random on crowds and pedestrians, killing scores of innocent Danes, including women and children. In retaliation, the entire country went on strike.

As with all spontaneous mass movements, no one knows exactly how and where the general strike started. Some authorities are of the opinion that it started when the ten thousand workers at Burmeister & Wain, Denmark's largest shipbuilding concern, quit work at noon on July 26, 1944, as a protest against the increasing German violence. Others think its beginning was in Istedgade, a street in the heart of Copenhagen's working-class district, when on the evening of July 26 a bareheaded woman ran through the streets screaming, "They have shot my husband! They have shot my husband! He hasn't done anything!"[11] Outside the front door of her house lay the body of her husband, a Copenhagen worker, shot down from behind by a member of the Schalburg Corps. According to an eyewitness account: "In a flash the whole street was full of angered Danes, busily occupied in erecting barricades to prevent the

Schalburg Nazis and the Germans from again showing their faces at this spot. From Istedgade the disturbances spread to other streets in the Vesterbro district and gradually throughout Copenhagen."[12]

Whether or not the general strike actually started in Istedgade, there is no doubt that Istedgade played a key role in its effectiveness. At first the barricades that were built consisted of torn-up paving stones, beds, mattresses and furniture. Later, automobiles and trolley cars were overturned to make the barricades more formidable. Banners were raised over the barricades reading: "Istedgade Never Gives In!" The Germans opened fire, killing several Danes, but they were unable to penetrate the barricades. The ruthlessness of the Germans made the Danes react in a manner quite untypical of them. A collaborator was spotted, pounced upon and had all of his clothes ripped off. A woman cried out that she would see to it that he would be unable to burden the earth with children of his kind, and, with her sewing scissors, cut off his testicles. Women in the district known to have fraternized with German soldiers were seized, their clothes torn off, their hair shaved and large swastikas painted on their naked bodies. At night huge bonfires were started on the street to violate the blackout. These bonfires were seen in other parts of the city, and before the end of the strike there were to be as many as five thousand bonfires burning nightly in Copenhagen.

On Tuesday, June 27, the strike movement began to spread to other large industrial concerns throughout Copenhagen, and even the shops began to close at noon. The Germans issued a stern warning against the shutdown, promising a reign of terror if it continued. On Wednesday no one showed up for work in the factories, offices or stores of Copenhagen, and the reign of terror began. The Germans, aided by the Schalburg Corps and a special group formed to work in conjunction with the Gestapo, known as the *Hilfs-Polizei*, or *Hipos*, began firing at random into Danish crowds and through the windows of Danish homes. Over a hundred Danes were killed, nearly a

thousand wounded. On Thursday the Germans executed eight
Danish patriots. In reply, the workers issued a call for an un-
limited extension of the now 100 percent effective strike. On
Friday the Germans announced their intention to starve Copenhagen. All gas, water and electricity were cut off from Danish
homes, and all roads leading into Copenhagen were blocked to
prevent food supplies from reaching the city. As a result of the
German announcement of these measures, the strike began to
spread throughout the country. At least twenty provincial
towns, including Aarhus, Denmark's second-largest city, followed the example of the capital and went on strike. In Copenhagen itself, the newly formed secret organization of underground leaders known as the Freedom Council announced that
while it had not instigated the strike, it now felt that it was its
duty to take control and lead it to a successful conclusion. Asking the population to continue the strike, the Freedom Council
demanded that the Germans meet four conditions before the
strike could be called off: (1) the Schalburg Corps to be ex-
pelled from the country; (2) the curfew and martial law to be
abolished; (3) traffic to and from Copenhagen to be re-opened;
(4) no reprisals for the strike.

For several days the strike and its consequent violence continued unabated. More barricades sprang up throughout Copenhagen and the provincial cities. At night the Danes sat in the
dark, sharing among themselves their carefully rationed food,
and staying away from their windows, through which a capricious burst of gunfire might come at any moment.

On July 3 the Germans issued a proclamation promising that
if the strike were halted they would agree to the Council's
demands. The Freedom Council then asked the people to return
to work. Many returned the following day, and by July 5
everyone was back on the job.

The Times of London said of the general strike: "The history of the European underground movement, so rich in
examples of the triumph of an organized popular action against

apparently invincible power, contains no instance of so complete and impressive a victory as that which the Danes have now won."

The resistance of the Danes to the Germans extended to every profession in Denmark, including the police. While in other occupied countries the Germans often found the local police willing helpers in their persecution of the Jews and other outrages, in Denmark the Germans found the Danish police to be almost totally uncooperative. Indeed, it was known that the Danish police played a large role in the rescue of the Jews and, later, in sabotage actions against the Germans. For this reason, the Germans attempted to arrest the entire Danish police force. On September 19, 1944, the Germans set off a false air-raid alarm, knowing that this would bring the entire police corps to its posts. The Wehrmacht then swooped down upon the Danish police and arrested several thousand of them. Over half of the Danish police managed to escape and join the underground. Those captured were sent to Neuengamme and Buchenwald. Elie Wiesel, a Hungarian prisoner at Buchenwald, recalled their arrival: "They were wonderful, these Danish policemen. Their courage, dignity and humanity were an inspiration to us, renewing our will to live. As we got to know them we saw that they were the salt of the earth." A large percentage of them were never to return to Denmark. Over six hundred of them were killed and cremated. Their ashes were returned to Denmark in common urns.

In resisting the Germans, 3,213 Danes were killed. After the war, the bodies of 199 Danish patriots murdered by the Germans were found in a common grave at Ryvangen in Copenhagen. This spot has been turned into a burial place for the victims and a memorial park for all Danes who died opposing the German tyranny. It is consecrated with these words from the Old Testament: "You stand here on holy ground."

Chapter 20 IN SWEDEN

It's comin' yet for a' that
When man to man, the world o'er,
Shall brithers be for a' that.

—ROBERT BURNS

IN 1943 THE DANISH AMBASSADOR to the United States was Henrik Kauffmann. When he first received word of the German plan to round up the Jews in Denmark, he was in Montreal at a breakfast meeting with the city's mayor. He immediately closeted himself in his room and began drafting a letter to Cordell Hull, the United States secretary of state. After a while, a Canadian representative appeared to inform him that the mayor had been waiting for him for over an hour.

"He will have to wait even longer," was Mr. Kauffmann's reply. "This is more important."[1] It was not until after he had finished writing the letter and had dispatched it that he set out to see the mayor. This is what Mr. Kauffmann wrote to the Secretary of State:

SIR:

According to press reports that have just reached this Legation, one of the first acts of the newly appointed military dictator in occupied Denmark was, on personal orders from Adolf Hitler, to start the deportation of the Danish Jews.

I greatly fear that very little can be done from here to come to the aid of these, my fellow citizens, in their hour of affliction. I want, however, to give you the assurance, Mr. Secretary, that any measures the American Government might deem feasible and appropriate to take in an attempt to afford protection to the Danish Jewish population, or to alleviate their fate and the threat against their lives, will have my full and unconditional support. As far as financial responsibilities may be involved, I undertake the guaranty towards your Government, or any other Government that may incur expenses in the effort to bring help to Danish Jews or other Danish nationals persecuted by the Nazis, to reimburse such expenses out of the Danish public funds under my control in this country. In making this declaration I know I am acting in line with the wish of the people of Denmark.

I should be grateful for an early opportunity to discuss with you, Sir, what it may be possible to do in order to render assistance to my nationals and to protect them against the dangers threatening their existence.

Receive, Sir, the assurance of my highest consideration.

In reply to Mr. Kauffmann's letter, the United States State Department, on the odd excuse that public knowledge of the Ambassador's offer would work to the disadvantage of the Jews, asked the Danish Ambassador to keep the contents of his letter secret. However, Mr. Kauffmann immediately cabled the Swedish Foreign Ministry in Stockholm to notify them that should Sweden accept the Danish Jews, he would put at their disposal the funds to underwrite all costs involved. In addition, he contacted leaders of the American Jewish community, including Rabbi Stephen S. Wise, to make known to them his offer and to assure them that he would do everything he could to aid their coreligionists in Denmark. Rabbi Wise was so moved by Mr. Kauffmann's proposal that he later described it to a friend as one of the most heart-warming acts of humanity which he, as a Jew, had ever experienced from a Christian.

When the German-controlled Danish authorities learned of

the offer which their ambassador to the United States had made without their authority, they dismissed him from office, denounced him as a traitor and ordered him to return to Denmark immediately to stand trial for treason. Mr. Kauffmann chose to remain in the United States, where he requested and received from the United States government recognition as the official representative of Free Denmark. One of his first acts in this capacity was to grant the United States temporary authority over Greenland. In return, Cordell Hull saw to it that Congress passed a special bill enabling Mr. Kauffmann at his discretion and for whatever use he deemed fit to free all Danish funds in the United States, including part of the gold stock of the Danish National Bank. This amounted to over twenty million dollars.

By this time Sweden had publicly announced her willingness to accept all Danish Jews, and many of them had already made their way there. Kauffmann was now in a position to offer Sweden funds to insure adequate care for the refugees. At the same time, he wanted to avoid, if possible, economic difficulties that might develop as the result of large-scale withdrawals from the public Danish funds. For this reason, working in conjunction with two American citizens of Danish extraction, Jean Hersholt, the well-known actor, and Leo Nathan, a New York furrier, Kauffmann attempted to raise part of the money for the refugees from American sources. On October 17, under the imprint of the Royal Danish Legation, Kauffmann circulated a letter to a wide variety of Jewish and non-Jewish individuals and organizations, asking for assistance. In it he pointed out that arrest and deportation of the Danish Jews "would—in fact—be identical with their destruction"* and that "this matter does not call upon Jews alone, but on all right-minded peoples, especially those of Danish descent." He added:

* It is interesting to note how many Allied government officials were not as well informed as Mr. Kauffmann. Some of these officials denied any knowledge of the tragic implications of the deportations as late as 1945.

"It is my hope that all Danes and Danish-Americans will consider it a duty of honor to help the Danish refugees in Sweden. I have reason to believe that the Danish-American population share my opinion that this is a matter that concerns us all."[2]

The response was gratifying. Individuals and organizations gave generously. Fur manufacturers contributed large sums of money, and the fur workers' union donated five hundred fur vests to be used by Danish seamen who had left Denmark to sail for the Allied cause.

As it turned out, no money had to be withdrawn from the Danish government's funds. Not only were American contributions generous, but the Swedish government itself contributed the handsome amount of five million dollars.[3] In addition, although the Jewish refugees generally arrived in Sweden penniless, with only the clothes on their backs, many of them quickly found jobs and were able to support themselves. In some cases, men who were accustomed to lifting nothing heavier than a fountain pen volunteered to go to the rugged northern regions of Sweden to cut timber. Inevitably, however, these would-be woodsmen collapsed under the strain and returned to Stockholm after several days in a state of complete physical exhaustion. More appropriate positions for these Jewish lawyers, teachers and clerks were to be found in refugee relief work. There was a great need for them in this capacity, but their roles in relief work occasionally engendered ill-feelings on the part of some of the non-Jewish refugees.

Of the 17,020 Danish refugees in Sweden, 9,114 belonged to the non-Jewish group.[4] The vast majority of these—saboteurs and resistance leaders who had been discovered by the Germans—arrived after the Jews. Several of them found it ironic that those whom they had helped to rescue were now heads of refugee camps and on the refugee clearing committees interviewing them. All in all, however, things went smoothly between Jewish and non-Jewish Danish refugees. After the dissipation of the initial resentment, there was no further sign of ill-will.

The Swedish government could not have been more cooperative toward the Danish refugees. Its generous financial contribution was matched only by the conscientious care it took to see that all of the refugees were properly housed, clothed and fed. In addition, the Swedish government formed special schools for the Danish children, supplying them with books and examination papers smuggled into the country from Denmark. Older students who had been at the University of Copenhagen had their examination papers smuggled back to Denmark to be graded by their professors at the University. In this way, no time was lost by the University students, six of whom received their law degrees from the University of Copenhagen while they were refugees in Sweden. Other students who preferred transferring to Swedish schools were permitted to do so. As quickly as possible, Danes were taken out of the refugee camps and placed in their own apartments in Stockholm and other cities. A special bureau was created to help find them jobs as well as housing. Swedish officials followed a rigorous policy of treating refugees of German or Polish origin in exactly the same fashion as they treated the Danes.

The Swedish government aided Pastor Borchsenius in setting up his Danish Church in Sweden, although the quarters they gave him for it caused him some embarrassment and annoyance. As Borchsenius described it:

"We found the entrance and started to climb up a worn stone staircase with a missing step. Through a ramshackle door we entered three small rooms. The beds were unmade and in a rather disgusting condition. I got hold of the landlady to ask why the place had not been cleaned up for our arrival. It was then that I found out that we were in a brothel. . . . It seems the police had suspected the enterprise and the owner had decided to stop the shop for some time and had offered the rooms to the Danish Refugee Service. And this was where I was supposed to establish a church office!

". . . we started to clean out the Augean stables. There was dirt enough, and, before our little office was finished, we had to throw several unmentionables out through the door.

"During the next few days some of the old clients of the shop kept appearing and asking, 'Isn't a certain lady supposed to live here?'

" 'Yes, but she's moved,' was the monotonous answer until the clients came to realize the change.

"Finally a resplendent sign was put on the door:

> Royal Danish Legation
> Refugee Office
> Danish Church in Sweden."[5]

Actually, very little time was spent by Pastor Borchsenius in his church. Most of the Pastor's energies went into traveling throughout Sweden lecturing to the Swedes on the nature of the war and the evils of anti-Semitism. Unfortunately, Pastor Borchsenius found that there was considerable need for him to lecture the Swedes on anti-Semitism.

While the attitude of the Swedish government toward the Danish refugees was impeccable, the same cannot be said for a number of Swedish individuals. In Malmø, which served as a clearing area for the refugees, Mendel Katlev and his family were disconcerted to find strong evidence of anti-Semitism on the part of the Swedes. "Why don't you Jews go back to where you came from?" was a rhetorical question they heard more than once.

Pinches Welner, a novelist, also encountered anti-Semitism in Malmø. In the evenings the refugees would meet in the city's two main squares—Stortorget and Gustaf Adolfs Torg—to discuss the latest news from Denmark. One particular evening they were discussing the friendliness with which the Swedish press had received them—a leading newspaper had editorialized

that the Danish Jews were an organic part of the Danish population and were among the most cultivated people in the world
—when a gang of young men appeared among them passing out
handbills. On the handbills were written five instructions:

1. Do not talk Yiddish.
2. Do not walk in groups.
3. Do not stop when walking.
4. Keep off the main streets and squares.
5. Stay home as much as possible.[6]

During the next few days, Welner and other refugees encountered groups of young men standing on street corners
throughout Malmø shouting: "Sweden for the Swedes! Sweden
for the Swedes!"

While some Swedes resented the arrival of the refugees,
others went out of their way to help them. Mrs. Rosa Bertman
of Hälsingborg was one of two Swedish women to have
received one of Denmark's highest awards, the Freedom Medal,
bestowed upon her by King Christian X for her activities in
behalf of the Danish refugees. In 1943, Mrs. Bertman, while
raising a boy of five and a girl of eight, worked at her husband's
clothing store. When the exodus from Denmark began, Mrs.
Bertman devoted her full energies day and night to help those
refugees who landed at Hälsingborg. During the first days of
October, before the Swedish government had an opportunity
to organize refugee relief efficiently, Mrs. Bertman sheltered
and fed dozens of them in her own house until other accommodations could be found for them. She convinced Evert
Ekblom, a hotel-owner, to house many of them at his hotel
without charge, and persuaded many private Swedish families
to accommodate the refugees. In addition, Mrs. Bertman
worked tirelessly to raise money and provide the refugees with
ration cards. Mrs. Bertman considered one of her most impor-

tant functions to be showing the refugees that they were welcome. Often this meant sitting up all night talking to them.
Even though they had successfully escaped the Nazis and were
now in a free, neutral country, many of them were sad and
depressed because they had left behind all of their possessions
and were in a strange land without means, relatives or friends.
Mrs. Bertman was a friend to hundreds of them.

Another good friend of the Jewish refugees was a police
commissioner of Hälsingborg, Carl Palm. As early as 1939,
when Germany invaded Poland, Palm felt that it would be
morally wrong for Sweden to try to remain neutral. He considered it obligatory for democratic countries to take an active
role in fighting dictatorships. When Denmark was invaded a
year later, Palm began working as an underground contact in
Sweden for those members of the Danish police force he knew
were anti-German. He supplied them with information which
he thought would be useful to the Allies, such as German troop
movements through Sweden to Norway.

With Palm's background of political activity, it was only
natural for him to want to help the Danish Jews. He remem-
bered well the first large batch of them who arrived at Hälsingborg:

"There were about two hundred of them, and among them
were dozens of women with babies in their arms. It was a sight
that at first seemed a nightmare to me. The babies and the
children were so still that I was sure they were dead. I couldn't
believe it. Why were the grownups all alive and all the children
dead? You see, I didn't know at that time that the children had
been given injections to make them sleep. I couldn't help myself, I started to cry. And with the tears running down my face
I screamed out loud my everlasting hatred of the Germans. The
people watching me must have thought that I was crazy."[7]

Palm set up a processing system for the Jews at the Town
Hall of Hälsingborg. Once processed, they were sent from

Hälsingborg to Malmø. One day, a group of Jews went on a sit-down strike in the Town Hall, refusing to go on to Malmø. Palm knew how very important it was for them to move on and to make room for new arrivals, but the refugees refused to move. They told Palm that it was Yom Kippur, the Day of Atonement, and that they could not travel for twenty-four hours. Palm telephoned the Chief Rabbi of Malmø and told him that the stubbornness of the orthodox Jews was upsetting the processing routine. The rabbi immediately journeyed to Hälsingborg and persuaded the orthodox Jews to accompany him back to Malmø.

Palm also organized censorship of the refugees' mail to Sweden. Dozens of postcards and letters written by the refugees to friends back in Denmark had to be destroyed by the censors, because in them the refugees carelessly wrote of their safe arrival in Sweden and thanked those Danes who had helped them to escape. "I hated to destroy their mail," explained Palm, "but if the Germans had gotten hold of the letters, they would have had the names and addresses of some of the most important underground leaders."

Palm worked closely with Mrs. Bertman and another Swedish police commissioner, Göte Friberg, in finding accommodations for the refugees. Many of them he housed in his own home. When the Elsinore Sewing Club was formed, Palm cooperated with Erling Kiær and Thomod Larsen.

Palm claimed that he helped the Jewish refugees out of his belief in the necessity to oppose actively all dictatorships, and out of a traditional dislike and distrust of the Germans. "Even today you have to watch the Germans," said Palm. "One of them alone may perhaps be all right. On occasion even two of them may be tolerable. But put three or more of them together and they immediately start singing 'Deutschland Uber Alles.'"

Still another Swede who was extremely active in behalf of the Danish refugees was Karl Gerhardt, a famous comedian in Sweden. In addition to contributing large sums of money toward their aid, he arranged for Jewish singers, actors and musicians to work in Swedish cafés and theaters.

Many of the Jewish refugees in Sweden, women as well as men, joined their fellow Danes in organizing an armed force to fight in the liberation of their country. Known as the Danish Brigade, and numbering five thousand, it received its training and equipment from the Swedish government. One of the first to join was Mrs. Ina Haxen. She had discovered that the man who had tortured her friend Peter P. Rohde was a Mr. Qvist, and she was more determined than ever to put to use her training in firing a gun to settle a personal score with Qvist as well as to aid in the liberation of her country.

Mogens Staffeldt, upon arrival in Sweden, went to work for the Danish Red Cross, compiling from memory lists of Danes he knew to be in German concentration camps. Later he became right-hand man to Ebbe Munch, head of the Danish underground in Sweden. Munch placed Staffeldt in charge of all illegal transportation between Denmark and Sweden.

Julius Margolinsky spent part of his time in Sweden compiling a statistical analysis of the Danish refugees.[8] Under the title "The Danish-Jewish Refugees in Sweden," he worked out twenty-one tables with commentaries showing the numerical relations between the Jewish and non-Jewish refugees from Denmark as to their age, sex and marital status. In addition, he registered all births, deaths and weddings that took place among the refugees during their stay in Sweden. He also charted the numerical proportion between the established Danish-Jewish families and those Jews who had immigrated from eastern Europe after 1904 and after 1933. Finally, his statistics detailed the mixed marriages before the escape from Denmark and during the stay of the refugees in Sweden.

It was quite an impressive statistical study. But after the war, when Margolinsky presented it to the Danish government, it was rejected. The Danish government pointed out that it did not doubt the accuracy of Mr. Margolinsky's statistics; it was simply not interested in any statistical study that classified people according to religion. Further evidence of this attitude on the part of the Danish government can be found in its officially commissioned history of the Danish refugees in Sweden, *De Danske Flygtninge I Sverige*, edited by Per Møller and Knud Secher. In it there is not a single reference to Jews. It deals only with *refugees*.

Chapter 21 VELKOMMEN TIL
DANMARK!

You shall grow and flourish and seed;
You are still too poor to die.

> —MORTEN NIELSEN,
> Danish poet killed by the Germans in
> 1943, when he was twenty-two years old

FRIDAY, APRIL 13, 1945, was a lucky day for the
Danish prisoners of Theresienstadt. An automobile flying the
Swedish flag arrived at the concentration camp. Its arrival was
not unexpected. On the previous day a clean-up program for
the camp had been ordered by the Germans. This usually
meant the imminent arrival of a Red Cross inspection commission from Sweden or Switzerland. While the men who
stepped out of the automobile were Swedish Red Cross officials,
their mission on this occasion was far more significant than an
inspection tour. At 8 P.M. the Danish prisoners were assembled
on the camp square and told the good news: through a special
arrangement concluded between Folke Bernadotte and Heinrich Himmler, all Danish prisoners were soon to be taken from
Theresienstadt to neutral Sweden. The prisoners were almost

too stunned to react. Rabbi M. Friediger described his own feelings upon receiving the information: "I told myself that if heaven opened its gates to me, the grandeur I would see there would make no greater impression upon me than this message. I remained perfectly motionless, paralyzed. . . . Was it once more a dream? One of my own, self-constructed dreams? No, it was reality."[1]

After the departure of the Swedish representatives, the Danes were reassembled and addressed by the S.S. The Germans confirmed the news that they had been given by the Swedish Red Cross officials, but listed three conditions. The Jews would be permitted to leave for Sweden only if they comported themselves in an exemplary manner until the date of departure, put the camp into neat order before they left and promised to tell everyone who questioned them before, during and after the trip to Sweden that their stay at Theresienstadt had been "productive and happy."[2] The prisoners quickly agreed to the three conditions.

Two days later a group of large Swedish buses with huge red crosses painted on their roofs and sides entered Theresienstadt. The Kørzens, Oppenheims, Cohens and Friedigers, together with all of the other Danish prisoners, handed over to the non-Danish prisoners all of their food packages and extra clothing. They then boarded the buses. An orchestra comprised of prisoners of various nationalities led by a German conductor played bright marches as the buses pulled away from the concentration camp grounds.

The destination of the Danes was Malmø, Sweden. To get there they had to pass first through north Germany and then through south Jutland and Copenhagen. Accompanying the Danes on the buses were Gestapo officers in civilian clothes. Passing through Germany, the Danes saw the destruction and ruin that the Nazis had wrought upon their own country. They could also see troops of new German recruits marching alongside the roads. These were companies of twelve- and thirteen-year-olds. The Gestapo officers aboard the buses lowered the shades each time they passed a heavily bombed area. The shades were raised and lowered so often that one of the Swedish bus drivers finally blurted out, "For God's sake, why don't you leave the shades alone. Leave them up or down, but leave them alone. If you continue to lower them each time we pass a place that's been destroyed, your arms will become sore long before we reach the border."

The Gestapo officers said nothing, but left the shades down. The passengers were too frightened to comment.

When the shades were finally raised, the buses had crossed the frontier into Denmark. Just beyond the frontier, the prisoners saw an incredibly stirring sight, a sight that was to be repeated with each town that they passed through on their way to Copenhagen—thousands of Danes of all ages were lined up along the road, waving Danish flags and joyously shouting, "*Velkommen til Danmark! Velkommen til Danmark!*"

Cilla Cohen turned to her husband. "Is this a holiday?" she asked. "Why all the crowds? Why all the flags?"

"Yes, it is a holiday," replied Mr. Cohen. "A very special holiday for *us*. They are here to greet *us*."

Suddenly the crowds lunged forward and surrounded the buses, forcing them to stop. While continuing to wave their Danish flags, to throw kisses and to chant, the people passed through the open bus windows bouquets of flowers, boxes of candy, chocolates, cigarettes and bottles of milk. The passengers were overwhelmed. One of them stood up and began singing the Danish national anthem, and all of the other passengers immediately took it up. This was too much for the Gestapo men. Brandishing their pistols, they warned the crowds to move away from the buses and ordered the bus drivers to continue.

Throughout the long drive to Copenhagen, the roads were filled with Danes joyously welcoming home their fellow countrymen.

In the town of Padborg, the passengers were allowed off the buses to wash and eat. The inhabitants of the town fought for the privilege of inviting their fellow countrymen into their homes.

The bus journey to Malmø continued. When the buses finally entered Copenhagen, there were literally hundreds of thousands of Danes in the streets to greet the prisoners. The cheering was deafening. The passengers were overjoyed. At the same time, they could not help but feel somewhat sad. The reason for the sadness was explained by one of the passengers, Ralph Oppenheim: "You felt wonderful leaving Theresienstadt, and felt even more wonderful seeing how your countrymen were welcoming you back home. But you were saddened by the thought that here you were going through your own country, passing through Copenhagen, your own city, and were not allowed to stop, but had to continue on to Sweden."

The hearty welcome given their fellow citizens by the inhabitants of Copenhagen did not meet with the Germans' approval. Through loudspeakers came an announcement that unless the noisy demonstration ceased, the prisoners would be sent back to Theresienstadt. The shouting, cheering and throwing of flowers into the buses stopped, but the people remained where they were. Silently, with broad smiles on their faces, they continued to wave their flags. The buses rolled on through the streets, finally reaching the docks, where the passengers boarded the ferries for Malmø. The Gestapo officers accompanied them aboard. It was not until the Danes were safe on Swedish soil and the Gestapo officers were on a boat headed back toward Copenhagen that the Danes were able to give full vent to their feelings. Together with the thousands of Danish refugees in Sweden who had come to Malmø to greet them, they laughed and they cried. Two months later, they were returned home.

On May 5, 1945, the British Army entered Copenhagen and the Germans surrendered. Later in the day, the first contingents of the Danish Brigade began arriving, but the fighting was already over. Mrs. Ina Haxen, in uniform, with loaded revolver, took leave of her company and sought out Qvist, the torturer of her friend Peter P. Rohde. She learned that Qvist had been liquidated and that Rohde was still alive and had been freed that very day. Mogens Staffeldt, arriving even before the Danish Brigade, went directly to his bookstore. There he learned that shortly after his escape to Sweden all of his clerks but one had been arrested by the Germans, but, following the German capitulation, they had been released from prison.

Toward the end of May, the Danish refugees began coming back from Sweden, and by the middle of July they were all home. Benjamin Slor, the wine merchant, found his apartment in better condition than when he had left it. Thanks to his friend Henri Smyth, it was newly painted and cleaned, and a four days' supply of food had been put in the refrigerator. In addition, he found that his clerks had continued to run his business in his absence, drawing only their normal weekly salaries and depositing the profits, which were sizable, to Slor's account, under a fictitious name.

Slor's case was typical of the way thousands of the refugees found their houses upon their return to Copenhagen. Neighbors and friends had not only painted and cleaned them, but, on the day of the refugees' return, had filled them with flowers. Hirsch Tschernia and his family were given a banquet by their neighbors the night of their return. As for the poorer refugees, money was contributed to help them return to normal life. Those whose apartments and houses had been destroyed by the Germans were given new homes by the government.

Many of the returning refugees found that during their absence even their household pets and plants had been cared for by their neighbors. Mr. and Mrs. Erik Hertz learned that while they were in Sweden their maid had entered their apartment several times a week to water their plants.

Possibly the only Dane to admit being less happy upon his

return to Denmark than he had been upon his arrival in Sweden was the parliamentary commissioner of Denmark, Stephan Hurwitz. "I arrived in Sweden," explained Mr. Hurwitz, "possessing only the clothes on my back. To be free of all possessions and responsibilities was one of the most wonderful feelings I have ever known. The day I returned to Denmark, on the other hand, I was quite disturbed because I found that while all of my other possessions were intact, one of my six thousand books was missing, a single volume from my highly prized seventy-two-volume collection of Voltaire. That's human nature for you."[3]

Mr. Hurwitz' reaction may have been true to human nature, but it was, of course, the exception to the rule. Virtually all of the Danish refugees remember their return home as the most glorious day of their lives. The significance of this reception has been made clear by Rabbi Melchior: "The people of other countries have let their Jews go before, and, perhaps, they were happy to get rid of them, especially when Jewish homes, property and money were involved. In such cases, saying 'Goodbye' was easier than saying 'Welcome back.' But when we returned, our fellow Danes did say 'welcome back.' And how they said it—emotionally, with open arms and hearts. Our homes, our businesses, our property and money had been taken care of and returned to us. In most cases we found our homes newly painted, and there were flowers on the table. You cannot imagine how happy it made us feel to be back home. The welcome we received from the King, from everybody, is the most important event in Danish-Jewish history."[4]

Chapter 22 WHY THE DANES?

*These groups enabled our townsfolk to come to grips
with the disease and convinced them that, now that
the plague was among us, it was up to them to do
whatever could be done to fight it. Since plague became in this way some men's duty, it revealed itself as
what it really was; that is, the concern of us all.*

—ALBERT CAMUS

THE DANISH PEOPLE WERE NOT ALONE in acting
heroically and effectively in saving their Jewish population. In
every country under Nazi control, including Germany, there
were individual acts of courage and humanity that constitute
a resounding *Yes!* to the question *Am I my brother's keeper?*
In Bulgaria, Italy and Holland these acts were numerous. But
it was only in Denmark that virtually the entire Jewish population of the country was saved. It was only in Denmark that
almost everyone, from King to fisherman, took an active role in
rescuing the Jews. It was only in Denmark that after World
War II *over 98.5 percent of the Jews were still alive.*[1]

Why? Why did the Danes behave so courageously and
honorably?

There is no one answer. There are many answers. And we

255

will never know all of them. If we could, we should be able to solve the problem of man's inhumanity to man. More important, we should be able to establish a formula for humanity. But it is worth examining some of the answers.

One important factor is Denmark's geographical proximity to neutral Sweden and the fact that after 1943 Sweden was willing to accept all refugees who reached her shores. The Danes at least had a refuge to which they could send their Jews. The same could not be said for the peoples of most of the other German-occupied countries.

Luck too played its part. The Danes were fortunate in that the German head of shipping operations in Copenhagen, Duckwitz, was so opposed to the Nazi persecution of the Jews that he was willing to risk his life by revealing to the Danes secret information about the preparations for the raid. Had the Danes not received Duckwitz' advance warning, they would have had little if any opportunity to act. And Duckwitz was not the only German in Denmark opposed to Nazi racism. Many of the Wehrmacht troops sent to occupy Denmark were older men, often in their forties and fifties. Unlike the younger Germans, they had no great belief in the New Order. In several instances Wehrmacht officers were known to have been uncooperative in the Gestapo's drive to arrest the Danish Jews. On one occasion, a Wehrmacht officer in Amager, upon being told by a subordinate that Jews were boarding fishing vessels in the harbor, was said to have replied, "These people are the Gestapo's responsibility, not ours. Now let me finish my drink in peace."[2]

For many Danes, the rescue of the Jews was primarily an act of protest against the German occupation. By the fall of 1943, the bestial character of Nazism was abundantly evident. The widely distributed publications of the Danish underground press had informed the people of German atrocities throughout the continent. In addition, large numbers of Danes were furious over the severe food rationing that had been imposed upon them by the Germans. They yearned for a chance to protest.

That opportunity came with the persecution of the Jews. Getting the Jews safely to Sweden was tantamount to slapping the faces of the Germans.

For many of the younger Danes, love of adventure was often the initial motivation. Because Germany had treated Denmark with kid gloves during the early years of the occupation, these Danish youths had little notion of the brutality with which the Germans carried out their reprisals. There was no Danish Lidice or Ouradour-sur-Glanes.

Leadership was certainly an important factor. The King, church leaders, the heads of the medical profession, student groups and business organizations set examples which inspired others to emulate their stubborn resistance.

The large numbers of intermarriages between Jews and Christians in Denmark must also be taken into account. Many Christian Danes had close Jewish relatives, and rare was the Danish Jew without a Christian member of the family to whom he could turn in distress. And if there were no relatives, there were almost always close friends. The Danish Jews were never forced to keep to themselves, and never voluntarily kept to themselves.

All of these factors played their part, but they do not answer the key question of why *the entire Danish population acted spontaneously to help.*

That answer is to be found in the Danish tradition of democracy.

To understand the differences between peoples, we must examine their traditions. It is difficult to find traditions more extreme than those of Denmark and Germany.

In Germany, crimes against the Jews were not originated by the Nazis. History shows that the Germans began early with their persecution of the Jews. Easter was celebrated in Mainz in 1283 by the killing of ten Jews by a Christian mob. Two years later, at Munich, another group of German Christians set fire to a synagogue and burned to death 180 Jews. In 1286,

at Oberwesel, a German mob killed forty Jews.[3] The pattern
continued well into the Middle Ages. The founder of Protes-
tantism, Martin Luther, demanded that Germany rid itself of
the Jews by seeing "that their synagogues or schools be set on
fire, their houses be broken up and destroyed . . . and they be
put under a roof or stable, like the gypsies. . . ."[4] With a
vulgarity matched only centuries later by Julius Streicher,
Martin Luther gave his followers this example of Jew-baiting:
"The Devil has eased himself and emptied his belly again—that
is a real halidom for Jews and would-be Jews, to kiss, batten
on, swill and adore; and then the Devil in his turn also devours
and swills what those good pupils spue and eject from above
and below. . . . The Devil, with his angelic snout, devours
what exudes from the oral and anal apertures of the Jews; this
is indeed his favorite dish, on which he battens like a sow
behind the hedge. . . ."[5]

Denmark, on the other hand, has no tradition of anti-
Semitism. As we have seen, the Danish Parliament in 1690
rejected the idea of establishing a ghetto in Copenhagen, calling
its very concept "an inhuman way of life." In 1814, all racial
and religious discrimination was declared illegal in Denmark.
The Danes who saved the Jews are products of a Danish tradition of democracy that has always found abhorrent any form
of racism.

To understand why the Danes acted as they did, one must
know that for centuries the Danish outlook in all areas of life
has been oriented toward humanitarianism, decency, concern
for all citizens. Denmark is one of the world's oldest democra-
cies, economically as well as politically, with emphasis on
equality as well as freedom. Education has long been of primary
importance, illiteracy nonexistent, and all schools, from kinder-
garten through the University are free. The University of
Copenhagen was established before Columbus set sail for the
Indies. The Danes' concern for all of the people is seen not
only in free education, but in the field of social security, in

WHY THE DANES? 259

which Denmark has long been a leader. Unemployment insurance, workmen's compensation, socialized medicine and old age pensions for every Danish citizen were a way of life in Denmark long before World War II. All of these things undoubtedly went into the shaping of the modern Dane, giving him confidence, belief in his own worth and dignity and a sense of responsibility toward his fellow countrymen.

What the Danes did was the natural response of a democratic people.

For the Danes, democratic action has never been a one-time affair. They have always striven to keep their traditions contemporary with the times. Thus in 1946, when the Sixth British Army parachute division was sent to Palestine, the Danish volunteers who had joined it during the war petitioned to be excused from fighting against the Jewish people.

Another example of the continual application of Danish moral principles occurred shortly after the Hungarian uprising of 1956. The Danes had provided homes for over a thousand Hungarian refugees and, much to their dismay, found that some of the refugees were openly anti-Semitic. One of the leaders of the group boasted that once his country was really free, "all of the Jews will be hanged." Not since the German occupation had the Danes been exposed to such racism. They decided to do something about it. Believing example to be the best teacher, they set out to instruct the refugees in the Danish concept of brotherhood. Tactfully, without fanfare or publicity, they organized groups of dinners for the Hungarians at private homes at which were present Jews as well as non-Jews. Hungarian goulash was served, and the hosts gave each refugee ten kroner toward his Christmas shopping. The results of these dinners, according to their organizers, were most gratifying. Genuine warmth of human feeling and the bringing together of people on common ground proved to be excellent antidotes for racial poison.

In Denmark, traditions past and present are the keepers of the flame. When the times demanded it, that flame burst forth with a brilliance to warm the hearts of mankind. What the Danes did in October 1943 in rescuing their fellow countrymen of the Jewish faith gave an added meaning to the first line of the Danish national anthem: *Der er et yndigt land*. Translated, it means "It is a lovely land."

COPENHAGEN, STOCKHOLM, NEW YORK

1962

ACKNOWLEDG-
MENTS AND NOTES

ACKNOWLEDGMENTS

I would like to thank Richard Siemanowski, television producer and, more important, friend, for making possible my first trip to Denmark. His judgment and taste were largely responsible for the success of our documentary film on the rescue of the Jews. A generous grant by B'nai B'rith and its Anti-Defamation League made possible my second and much more extended visit to Denmark. Arnold Forster, Benjamin Epstein and Oscar Cohen of the ADL were at all times encouraging and helpful. I am especially grateful to Label Katz, president of B'nai B'rith.

Neither the film nor the book would have been possible without the assistance of a young indefatigable Dane by the name of Benni Kørzen. On both projects he was an incredibly efficient contact man, researcher and translator. Other researchers and translators who were most helpful were Ulf Haxen, Barbro Boman, Bessie Helqvist and Karen Emanuel. Jack Baker translated several documents from the German.

Ole Barfoed, Julius Margolinsky, Mogens Staffeldt and Walter Emlington went out of their way to be of assistance with contacts and material. Others who gave generously of their time include Niels Bohr, Rabbi Marcus Melchior, Ina Haxen, Benjamin Slor, Cilla Cohen, Stephan Hurwitz, Arthur

Friediger, Ralph Oppenheim, Pinches Welner, Dr. K. H. Køster, Jens Lillelund, Professor and Mrs. Richard Ege, Ambassador Henrik Kauffmann, Leo Nathan, Captain and Mrs. Christian Kisling, Jørgen Knudsen, Rosa Krotoschinsky, Inge Jensen, Pastor Poul Borchsenius, Carl Næsh Hendriksen, Mendel Katlev, Magnus Ruben, Erling Kiær, Thomod Larsen, Børge Rønne, Ole Helweg, Peder Christopher Hansen, Axel Olsen, Mrs. Ellen Nielsen, Miss Elise Schmidt-Petersen, Henry Grünbaum, Benjamin Kørzen, Carl Palm, Rosa Bertman and Arne Sejr.

Johannes Laursen and C. H. W. Hasselriis of the Danish Information Office in New York were very helpful, as was Helmut Rückriegel of the German Information Office. The Israel government was most kind in sending me photostatic copies of documents introduced at the Eichmann trial pertaining to the German occupation of Denmark.

Constructive suggestions about the manuscript were made by my aunt, Minna Seitzman. I am deeply indebted to her for her advice and understanding.

I wish also to thank my agent, Georges Borchardt, who encouraged the project from the first, and my editor, Michael V. Korda, whose assistance was invaluable.

NOTES

Melchior's Statement

1. As told to the author by Rabbi Melchior and recorded by Rabbi Melchior in the author's documentary film "An Act of Faith," broadcast over the CBS Television Network, December 31, 1961.

Chapter 1

1. Unless otherwise indicated, all military facts and quotes in this chapter relative to Denmark are from *Denmark During the German Occupation,* a collection of eyewitness accounts edited by Børge Outze (Copenhagen: The Scandinavian Publishing Company, 1946).

2. David Lampe, *The Danish Resistance* (New York: Ballantine Books, 1960), p. 1.

3. Joachim Joesten, *Denmark's Day of Doom* (London: Victor Gallaway, 1939).

4. As reported to the author by the magazine's editor, Hans Bendix, now one of Denmark's leading political cartoonists.

5. William L. Shirer, *The Rise and Fall of the Third Reich* (New York: Simon and Schuster, 1960), p. 698.

6. From Himer's record of the interview in the secret German Army Archives, as cited in *The Rise and Fall of the Third Reich,* p. 700.

7. Norwegian State Archives, as cited in William L. Shirer, *The Challenge of Scandinavia* (Boston: Little, Brown, 1955), p. 38.

8. Supplied to the author by the Norwegian Embassy Information

Service, File 250 E. Confirmed in Shirer, *The Rise and Fall of the Third Reich*.

9. *Ibid.*, p. 711.

10. From the opening speech and legal argument of Attorney General Gideon Hausner in the Eichmann trial, *The Jerusalem Post*, Jerusalem, 1961, p. 126.

11. From documents introduced at the Eichmann trial, Jerusalem, May 11, 1961. The author is indebted to the Israeli government for supplying him not only with the stenographic minutes of the Eichmann trial, but with photostats of all documents relating to Denmark introduced at the Eichmann trial. Of special relevance are the affidavits of Mildner and von Thadden, documents T580, T582, T584, T585, T587, T588, T589.

Chapter 2

1. Raul Hilberg, *The Destruction of the European Jews* (London: W. H. Allen, 1961), pp. 357–358.

2. German Undersecretary of State Dr. Martin Luther to legation in Copenhagen, October 1942, NG–5121, as cited in Hilberg, *op. cit.*

3. Sonnleithner via Weizsächer to Luther, February 1, 1943, NG–5121, as cited in Hilberg, *op. cit.*

4. Document PS 2375, "Nazi Conspiracy and Aggression," U.S. Government Printing Office, Washington, D.C., 1946–48, Vol. V.

5. Introduced at Eichmann trial as document T580.

6. There is not a single shred of evidence to show that any of the stories of King Christian X and the yellow Star of David are true. The apocryphal nature of the stories is attested to by Danish historians Per Hæstrup and Ole Barfoed, leading authorities on this period, as well as by Rabbi Melchior, librarian Julius Margolinsky, newspaper editor Børge Outze, and other authorities on the Danish Jews under the occupation. Furthermore, Nuremberg trial (NG–5121) and Eichmann trial (T580) documents establish that the German Foreign Ministry rejected the introduction of the Nuremberg decrees, including the wearing of the yellow Star of David, for Denmark. Nevertheless, that King Christian X was implacably opposed to anti-Semitism is firmly established. On the wall of Rabbi Melchior's apartment in Copenhagen hangs one of his proudest possessions, a letter he received from King Christian X on December 31, 1941, several days after the Germans had unsuccessfully attempted to set fire to the Copenhagen synagogue. The King wrote: "I have heard about the attempted fire at the Synagogue, and I am very happy that there was only slight

damage. I beg you to give my congratulations and best wishes for the
New Year to your congregation." Also see letter he wrote to Werner
Best, as cited in Chapter 5.

Chapter 3

1. Exhibit 1503, filed April 2, 1946, before the International Military
Tribunal, Nuremberg. In addition, affidavit of Rudolf Mildner, introduced at Eichmann trial as document T585.
2. Testimony of Paul Ernst Kanstein of the German legation at
Copenhagen, April 29, 1947, NG–5208, as cited in Hilberg, *op. cit.*
3. All military documents in this chapter are from Outze, *op. cit.*
4. Shirer, *The Challenge of Scandinavia*, p. 236.
5. *The Danish Toulon*, published by His Majesty's Stationery Office in behalf of the Danish Council in London, 1944.
6. Case XI, NG–3923, as cited in Gerald Reitlinger, *The Final
Solution* (New York: A. S. Barnes, 1961), p. 347.
7. Sonnleithner via Steengracht to Hencke, September 8, 1943,
NG–5121.

Chapter 4

1. The facts about Duckwitz are derived from several sources: the
account written by the late Prime Minister Hans Hedtoft himself as
the introduction to Aage Bertelsen, *October '43* (New York: G. P.
Putnam's Sons, 1954), pp. 16–19; the author's correspondence with
Duckwitz; an article in the May 14, 1961 issue of *Der Stern*, which
Duckwitz assured the author was accurate; affidavits in the possession
of historian Ole Barfoed; and testimony from the trial of Werner
Best in Copenhagen, 1945, at which Duckwitz was a witness.
2. Letters, telegrams, memoranda, etc., from secret German Army
Archives, documenting what transpired among the Germans in Den-
mark during this period can be found in Reitlinger, *op. cit.*, and
Hilberg, *op. cit.*
3. As told to the author by librarian Julius Margolinsky, and confirmed by Rabbi Melchior.

Chapter 5

1. As told to the author by Rabbi Melchior.
2. As told to the author by Jørgen Knudsen.

3. The accounts of Professor Richard Ege, Jens Lillelund, Mogens Staffeldt and Carl Næsh Hendriksen are all the result of the author's interviews with these widely acknowledged resistance leaders.

4. As told to the author by Abram Krotoschinsky's daughter, Rosa.

5. Archives, Danish Royal Library.

6. As told to the author by Mendel Katlev.

7. As told to the author by Magnus Ruben.

8. Memorandum by Svenningsen, October 2, 1943, NG–5208, as cited in Hilberg, *op. cit.*, p. 362.

9. The accounts of the German raid are derived from Werner Best's testimony at his trial, and the affidavits of von Thadden and Mildner introduced at the Nuremberg and Eichmann trials. See note 11, Chapter 1.

10. *Ibid.*

Chapter 6

1. Accounts had been carried in the illegal Danish newspaper, *Free Denmark*, and had also appeared in the pro-Allied Swedish newspaper, edited by Torgny Segerstedt. Copies are to be found in the archives of the Danish Resistance Museum.

2. Told to the author by an eyewitness, journalist Børge Rønne.

3. Archives, Royal Danish Library.

4. Bertelsen, *op. cit.* In addition, the author talked to Mr. Bertelsen.

5. Told to the author by Captain and Mrs. Kisling, corroborated by leading members of the Danish resistance. Mogens Staffeldt referred to Captain Kisling as "one of the finest among us."

6. *Den Hvide Brigade* ("The White Brigade"), edited by Aage Svendstorp (Copenhagen: Carl Allers, 1946), tells the story of the role of the Danish physicians during the German occupation.

7. Steengracht to von Sonnleithner, NG–4093, as cited in Reitlinger, *op. cit.*, p. 350, and Hilberg, *op. cit.*, p. 362.

8. Shirer, *The Challenge of Scandinavia.*

9. The incredible account of the role played by Niels Bohr in getting Sweden to announce her willingness to give refuge to all Danish Jewish refugees who reached her shores was told to the author by Niels Bohr himself. In addition, the story was corroborated by Danish journalist Vilhelm Slomann, who has reported extensively on the matter. A less detailed account can be found in Lampe, *op. cit.*

Chapter 7

1. As reported to the author by Per Hækkerup, now Foreign Minister of Denmark.

2. Archives, Danish Resistance Museum.
3. As told to the author by Stig Hansen's daughter Ingrid.
4. As reported to the author by refugees and resistance people who had contact with these fishermen.
5. As reported to the author by fisherman Peder Christopher Hansen.
6. As reported to the author by fisherman Axel Olsen.
7. As reported to the author by Rabbi Melchior.

Chapter 8

1. As reported to the author by Staffeldt, Lillelund and Truelsen.
2–4. As reported to the author by Lillelund.

Chapter 9

1. As told to the author by Dr. Karl Henry Køster.
2. Upon examination, it was discovered that the saboteur had a large ulcer, which both bullets had pierced when he was shot.
3. As told to the author by Dr. Karl Henry Køster and Dr. Ole Secher. Corroborated in Svendstorp, *op. cit.*
4. As told to the author by Nurse Jansen. Corroborated in Svendstorp, *op. cit.*
5. Svendstorp, *op. cit.*
6. Lampe, *op. cit.*, p. 58.
7. As told to the author by Dr. Køster. The statements by Dr. Secher, Nurse Jansen and Jørgen Knudsen were recorded by them in the author's documentary film on the Danish rescue of the Jews, "An Act of Faith."
8. As told to the author by Mrs. Køster.
9. Svendstorp, *op. cit.*, p. 175.

Chapter 10

1. As told to the author by Mrs. Ina Haxen.
2. From an account written by Mrs. Ina Haxen for the Royal Archives. (Most of Mrs. Haxen's story, however, is derived from the author's interviews with her.)
3. As told to the author by Professor Ege and Mrs. Ege.

4. Jørgen Gersfelt, *Sådan Narrade Vi Gestapo* (Copenhagen: Gly-
dendal, 1945).
5. Bertelsen, *op. cit.*, pp. 33–7.
6. *Ibid.*

Chapter 11

1. The material on the Lyngby Group is from Bertelsen, *op. cit.*
For full details of the Lyngby Group, the author recommends this
excellent little book. The facts of Mrs. Bertelsen's arrest and imprisonment are from an account written by herself as a separate chapter in her husband's book.

Chapter 12

1–3. Footnotes 1–3, as well as most of the material in this chapter,
are based upon interviews the author had with the key living members of the Elsinore Sewing Club—Børge Rønne, Erling Kiær,
Thomod Larsen, Ove Bruhn and Dr. Jørgen Gersfelt. Additional
material comes from the books written by Erling Kiær and Dr. Jørgen Gersfelt, as cited below.
4. Gersfelt, *op. cit.*
5. *Ibid.*
6. Erling Kiær, *Med Gestapo I Kølvandet* (Copenhagen: Frimodts
Forlag, 1946).
7. Gersfelt, *op. cit.*
8. Kiær, *op. cit.*

Chapter 13

1. Most of the material in this chapter is derived from interviews
the author had with Ole Helweg and Erik Stærmose.
2. Dansk-Svensk Flygtningetjenestes Arkiv, 1944, Stockholm.
3. *Gaa Til Modstand*, edited by Hans Jørgen Lembourn (Copenhagen: Det Schønbergske Forlag, 1961), p. 55, the chapter "Højst
Uvelkommen" by Leif B. Hendil.
4. As told to the author by Ettie Henriques.
5. As told to the author by Mr. and Mrs. Tesdorpf.

Chapter 14

1. Philip Friedman, *Their Brothers' Keepers* (New York: Crown Publishers, Inc., 1957), p. 156, contains a brief reference to "The Shooting Priest." Practically all of the material for this chapter, however, is derived from the author's interviews with Pastor Borchsenius, his daughter and several of the pastor's friends.

Chapter 15

1. As told to the author by Mrs. Ellen Nielsen.
2. As told to the author by Miss Elise Schmidt-Petersen.

Chapter 16

1. As told to the author by Benjamin Slor.

Chapter 17

1. As told to the author by the member of the Ministry of Finance involved. He requested that his name not be mentioned.
2. As told to the author by Mrs. Inge Jensen and recorded in the author's documentary film "An Act of Faith."
3-4. As told to the author by Mr. and Mrs. Mendel Katlev.
5. As told to the author by Carl Næsh Hendriksen.
6. As told to the author by Henry Grünbaum.

Chapter 18

1. Most of the material in this chapter relating to Ralph Oppenheim comes from the author's interviews with him. Some of the material is taken from Mr. Oppenheim's book, *Det Skulle Saa Være* (Copenhagen: 1945).
2. As told to the author by Mr. and Mrs. Benjamin Korzen.
3. As told to the author by Mrs. Cilla Cohen. In addition, some of Mrs. Cohen's story comes from her book, *En Jødisk Families Saga* (Copenhagen: Nyt Nordisk Forlag Arnold Busck, 1960).
4. H. G. Adler, *Theresienstadt 1941-1945* (Tübingen, Germany: J. C. B. Mohr, 1958).

5. M. Friediger, *Theresienstadt* (Copenhagen: 1945).
6. H. G. Adler, *Die Verheimlichte Wahrheit* (Tübingen, Germany: J. C. B. Mohr, 1958). (This is the companion volume to Adler's other volume cited above.)
7. Oppenheim, *op. cit.*
8. *Ibid.*
9. *Ibid.*
10. Cohen, *op. cit.*
11. As told to the author by Arthur Friediger.
12. Malcolm Hay, *Europe and the Jews* (New York: Beacon Press, 1961), p. 302.
13. *Ibid.*
14. Cohen, *op. cit.*
15. Adler, *Theresienstadt 1941–1945.*
16. Friediger, *op. cit.*
17. As told to the author by Mr. Leo Nathan.

Chapter 19

1. As told to the author by Ole Lippman and recorded in the author's documentary film "An Act of Faith."
2. Ole Barfoed, report on the effect of the Jewish persecution on the Danish resistance.
3. As told to the author by Christian Kisling and reported in an address by Kisling to the Freeport Temple, Freeport, N.Y., 1960.
4. As told to the author by Jørgen Knudsen.
5. Outze, *op. cit.*
6. Archives, Danish Resistance Museum.
7. Jens Lillelund, *When John Was Taken* (Copenhagen: 1946), p. 104.
8. As told to the author by Mogens Staffeldt.
9. As told to the author by Jens Lillelund.
10. As told to the author by Ina Haxen.
11. Holger Hørsholt Hansen, *Triumph in Disaster* (London: 1945), p. 11.
12. Vilhelm Bergstrøm, *Istedgade Overgiver Sig Aldrig* (Copenhagen: 1961).

Chapter 20

1. As told to the author by Mr. Kauffmann.
2. From circular letter from the Danish Embassy in Washington, dated October 17, 1943.

3. As reported to the author by Aage Hessellund-Jensen, permanent ambassador of Denmark to the United Nations, and, in 1943–45, in charge of the refugee problem in Sweden.

4. From Julius Margolinsky, "The Danish-Jewish Refugees in Sweden, 1943–1945," a statistical study.

5. Poul Borchsenius, *Udlændigheds Dage* (Copenhagen: Hasselbach Forlag, 1946).

6. As told to the author by Pinches Welner, and reported in his book, *I Hine Dage* (Copenhagen: Thanning & Appel, 1949).

7. As told to the author by Police Commissioner Carl Palm.

8. According to Margolinsky's statistical study, as of February 1, 1945, 17,020 refugees from Denmark had arrived in Sweden. Of these, 9,114 belonged to the non-Jewish group. They included members of the resistance movement, fishermen, members of the Army, Navy and Police. The "Jewish Group" numbered 7,806, including 686 non-Jews married to Jews.

Chapter 21

1. Friediger, *op. cit.*
2. As told to the author by Cilla Cohen.
3. As told to the author by Stephan Hurwitz.
4. As told to the author by Rabbi Melchior and recorded in the author's documentary film "An Act of Faith."

Chapter 22

1. According to statistics compiled by Mrs. Yahil of Yad Vashem, the official center in Israel for the documentation of Nazi genocide, 54 of the 472 Danish Jews sent to Theresienstadt died there, one was deported to Auschwitz, 20 died during the flight to Sweden and 20 committed suicide during the early days of October 1943.

2. Lampe, *op. cit.,* p. 58.
3. Hay, *op. cit.,* p. 127.
4. Shirer, *The Rise and Fall of the Third Reich*, p. 236.
5. Hay, *op. cit.,* p. 169.

Index